Guide to Producing a Fashion Show

Judith C. Everett
Northern Arizona University

Kristen K. Swanson

Original Photography
Chris Everett

FAIRCHILD PUBLICATIONS
NEW YORK

Contents

Preface

The fashion show should be an entertaining and rewarding experience for the show participants and audience. It is an exciting and theatrical presentation of apparel and accessories on live models conducted on many market levels—from the haute couture designers, presenting their latest innovations, to the ultimate consumer extravaganza held by community groups and retail stores. The purpose of *Guide to Producing a Fashion Show* is to lead individuals through the process of planning and presenting a fashion show, and to outline the steps necessary for organizing a successful event.

FEATURES

We begin with a discussion on the background and development of the various types of fashion shows. This framework includes the primary purpose of producing a show—to sell merchandise. The first part of the book also traces the history of the fashion show through a review of the designers, special events, and associations that influenced its advancement. European fashion shows have set the pace for innovative and theatrical shows. The unique styles of the French, Italian and British retailers and designers—couture and ready-to-wear—are thoroughly reported.

The next section of the book outlines the steps in planning the fashion show beginning with the first stages of planning—establishing the audience, type of show, site, theme and budget. Publicity and advertising are fully outlined. Preparation of press materials and advertising for newspapers, magazines, television and radio are investigated. We have provided examples of press releases and photographs as well as step-by-step instructions on how to write press releases to assist fashion show planners with this activity.

The merchandise selection process involves pulling, fitting and preparing merchandise. Grouping merchandise in order to plan the fashion show lineup to fit the theme is also part of this activity and is fully examined. The role of the individuals who display the merchandise—models—is an important feature of how the show looks. Therefore selecting and training models is crucial. We have considered the advantages and differences between using professional or amateur models in a fashion show and the responsibilities of all the models during the fitting, rehearsal and show.

Determining whether or not to use a commentator and commentary is the focus of Chapter 8. If commentary is to be used, techniques and examples of how to write good and avoid bad commentary are provided. The theatrical stage and runway can enhance the image or theme established in the early stages of planning. Distinct patterns for runways, seating arrangements, the appropriate use of lighting and props are featured.

The last portion of the book deals with choreography that sets the dramatic opening, pace and finale for the models. Also the selection of music, live or taped, to enhance the mood of the show is addressed. The rehearsal prepares all of the individuals for a professional presentation. Here problems are ironed out and the stage is set for the actual show.

All of the advance preparation pays off on the day of the show. Participants are excited to see everything pulled together, finally having the opportunity to introduce the show to the target audience. The thrill of all activities coming together results in a truly rewarding experience for the fashion show organizers, models, designers, technical staff, and audience. We also discuss the often neglected portion of producing a fashion show—striking the stage and returning merchandise to the designers, manufacturers or retailers. Another responsibility at this point is addressed—sending thank you notes and paying promptly for services.

The last chapter of *Guide to Producing a Fashion Show* outlines the final step in fashion show production—the evaluation process. This much overlooked step in fashion show production is really the first step for the production of the next fashion show. Each time a fashion show is presented, the participants learn how to make the next show even better.

Producing a fashion show is a hands-on learning experience. It is our hope that the techniques discussed throughout this book will provide a foundation for fashion show planners to organize this enormous project and that the behind-the-scenes photographs support and enhance this information. This in-depth study of fashion show production will serve as a valuable tool for fashion professionals, instructors and students of design, merchandising, and modeling, and civic or community leaders, giving them a view of all the aspects of this dramatic and exciting event. It will interest anyone who wants to know more about *how to produce a fashion show!*

1993

Judith C. Everett
Kristen K. Swanson

Acknowledgments

The authors wish to thank the many business associates, students, personal friends, and family who helped to make working on this project a pleasurable and rewarding experience. Additional thanks need to go to the reviewers—Diane Ellis, Marsha Stein, Sharon E. Tabaca, Janice Threw—whose suggestions were extremely beneficial. We appreciate all of the support from those individuals who were eager to answer questions, give counsel, review chapters and provide entrance backstage to many of their fashion shows.

A special thanks to the following people: Wendy Cholfin, Cholfin & Taylor Productions, Inc., Phoenix, Arizona; Kim Dawson, Kim Dawson Agency, Dallas Apparel Mart; Judy Edwards, Robert Black Agency, Tempe, Arizona; Karie Farrally, Special Events Director, Broadway Southwest; Bernie Goldstein, President, Dillard's Southwest Division; Lynette Harrison, *W*, Fairchild Publications; Milena Jovonic, Relations Clientele Internationale, Galeries Lafayette (Paris); Tony Keiser, Designer for Grey Elk Studio, Flagstaff, Arizona; Sally Liebig, Director, Flagstaff Winterfest, Arizona; Bob Mackie, Designer; Lee Merkle-Kemper, Special Events Director, Dillard's Southwest Division; Albert Nipon, Chief Executive Officer, Albert Nipon; Luciana Polacco, Director of Marketing, Laura Biagiotti, Milan; Beatrice Riordan, Flagstaff Symphony Guild, Flagstaff, Arizonia.

We have gained much by working with all of our students. These particular students served as inspiration and research assistants for this project. Thank you to Angel Gibson, Lynne Gilmore, Betsy Heimerl, Natalie Martin, and Ronnie Silverman.

Olga Kontzias, editor, at Fairchild Publications for keeping us on track. Without her guidance and enthusiasm this project would not have been completed.

Our mothers, Norma Culbertson and Bonnie Swanson, gave us a great foundation and appreciation of clothing. Thank you for your inspiration and encouragement.

Our husbands, Chris Everett and James Power. Thank you for putting up with the endless hours of fashion show talk and competing to use the computer. Chris served as our photographer and James contributed support when we needed to work on the computer.

Guide to Producing a Fashion Show

The Development of the Fashion Show

Every creative element of theatrical and modern entertainment media is used in a fashion show to present the latest colors, fabrics and fashion trends in apparel, and accessories, on live models to an audience. Certainly an advantage of seeing merchandise in an exciting live presentation is that the audience can become involved. They are not seeing a "representation" of a garment in a photograph or in an illustration from an advertisement, nor are they viewing a garment on a hanger. A model on the runway is wearing all the elements of apparel and accessories. The audience can react to the total look of an outfit and visualize how they might look wearing the newest and latest developments from the fashion world.

FASHION SHOWS SELL MERCHANDISE

After designers or manufacturers create garments, accessories or beauty products, promotion and merchandising contribute to the ultimate goal of selling these products. Fashion shows are produced with one primary purpose—to sell merchandise to consumers at all marketing levels from people working in the industry (designers, manufacturers, retailers) to fashion-conscious shoppers. The fashion show helps to make an authoritative visual statement about fashion, making it one of the most exciting and dramatic forms of sales promotion.

Sales promotion is defined as any activity to help deliver the product from the producer to consumer, and is a necessary function for the creators and distributors of fashion items. Other promotional activities include: advertising, personal selling, publicity, public relations, special events, and visual merchandising.

The three major market levels for promotional activities are national, trade and retail. National promotion involves primary and secondary resources (manufacturers) directing sales promotion activities toward the ultimate consumer. Primary resources are the producers of raw materials. These primary producers typically include textile fiber and fabric firms. Secondary resources in the apparel industry generally are the clothing and accessory manufacturers. National promotion is used to pre-sell the consumer. It is not uncommon for a primary or secondary manufacturer to cooperatively produce a fashion show with a retailer to attract the consumer. Several firms participate or financially support cooperative, or co-op, promotion in the presentation of a show.

Trade promotion activities promote products from one business to another. This type of promotional activity takes a product from a primary resource to a secondary resource, a textile mill to a clothing manufacturer. It may also promote products from a secondary producer to a retailer.

Retail promotion typically involves stores promoting their products to consumers. Retailers, the main distributors of fashion items, focus their sales promotion efforts on their target consumers. Retail organizations are considered tertiary resources

ADDITIONAL REASONS FOR PRODUCING FASHION SHOWS

Fashion-related organizations stage fashion shows for many reasons other than to sell merchandise. The most current fashion information such as the latest trends in apparel, silhouettes, fabrics, color, or services is transmitted to customers through this entertaining format.

Fashion shows are a type of sales promotion that involve presenting merchandise on live models to consumers. *(WWD)*

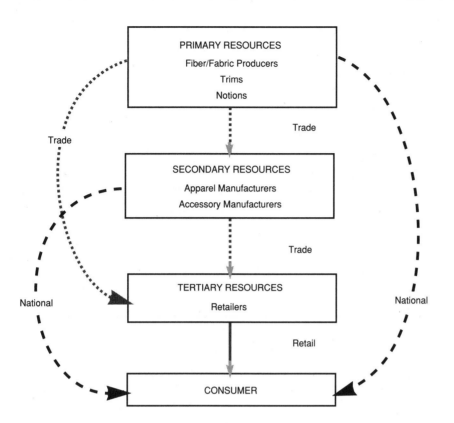

Figure 1-1
Channels of Sales
Distribution

Fashion organizations want to attract new customers, build traffic, and encourage current customers to return. Retailers can use fashion shows to solidify the store's position as a fashion authority and leader in the community and promote goodwill with local, regional or national patrons. A new product or line of merchandise may be introduced to customers through a fashion show.

In order to enhance a store's image as a fashion leader and increase sales for designer merchandise, the designer of the line may be invited to the store. For example Albert Nipon was the featured guest at an in-store formal fashion show and trunk show held at Dillard's Department Store, Southwest Division. The show was produced as a cooperative venture by the designer/manufacturer and the retail store.

When a manufacturing company introduces a secondary line targeting a specific type of customer such as Claiborne for Men or Elisabeth for Plus Sizes by Liz Claiborne, consumer or trade-oriented fashion shows are used to acquaint customers with the new product.

In addition to introducing new products, retail stores want to inform their customers about the depth, range, and variety of merchandise carried. This will enable the retailer to focus on the different brands carried, features of their private label merchandise, or a special merchandise offering.

Various organizations may wish to show current fashions for a business program, for a luncheon or annual meeting. Fund-raising activities for such charitable groups as the *American Heart Association*, *Muscular Dystrophy Association*, *Planned Parenthood*, art museums, or symphony guilds may include holding an entertaining fashion show. In order to promote goodwill within a community a retail store or group of stores may support charitable groups by lending clothing and accessories. In addition, a portion or all of the revenues from the ticket sales may be contributed to such charitable groups.

Fashion shows are also produced to provide training to at least two groups—fashion students and industry personnel. Nearly every fashion school produces an annual fashion show. This is the opportunity for students in apparel design to show their creations. Modeling students have an opportunity for a practical application of their presentation skills. Merchandising students learn the behind-the-scenes responsibilities for organization, selection of merchandise and models, promotion, presentation, and evaluation of the show.

Store personnel benefit from in-store produced training shows. During this type of show, the fashion office presents specific themes of merchandise that will be presented to customers during the next season. The training show helps to raise the staff's awareness of these specific trends and provides selling features to help market this merchandise. In-store training shows help to improve the attitude and morale of employees. They also help to increase their knowledge about products and upcoming events, greatly enhancing the personnel's loyalty and the store's identification as a fashion leader.

Fashion Show versus Style Show The contemporary name used in describing this live event presenting apparel and accessories on models is "fashion show." The use of the term "style show" is outmoded and old-fashioned. Fashion infers change and excitement. Style is something that remains static. Using the proper terminology is part of the professionalism of producing a fashion show.

EDUCATE CONSUMERS

SHOW LATEST FASHION TRENDS

ATTRACT NEW CUSTOMERS

BUILD TRAFFIC

ESTABLISH RETAILER AS A FASHION LEADER

PROMOTE GOODWILL

INTRODUCE NEW PRODUCTS

INTRODUCE A DESIGNER

INTRODUCE A THEME

DEMONSTRATE MERCHANDISE ASSORTMENTS

INDICATE SPECIAL MERCHANDISE OFFERING

DIFFERENTIATE BRANDS

PARTICIPATE IN A SPECIAL EVENT

TRAIN EMPLOYEES OR STUDENTS

Additional Reasons for Producing Fashion Shows

THE HISTORY OF THE FASHION SHOW

The fashion show has been used by ready-to-wear manufacturers from the start of the mass production industry as a sales promotion event. However, the true inventor of the modern runway fashion show—using live models—is unknown. One of the first methods used by dressmakers to transmit fashion information to reach potential consumers, that is the women of the royal courts, was to send fashion dolls. Fashion dolls were miniature scale figurines wearing replicas of the latest clothing. The dolls were also known as *puppets, dummies, little ladies,* or *fashion babies.* The earliest record of the fashion doll was in 1391 when the wife of Charles VI of France sent a full-size figure wearing the innovative French court fashions of the time to Queen Anne, wife of Richard II, King of England *(Corinth, 1970, p 11).* Although this was more like the modern day mannequin, it was called a fashion doll. Queen Anne was able to wear the garment immediately instead of having it reproduced from a miniature scale doll as was the common practice later.

Shipping dolls wearing the latest fashion trends from one royal court to another was a common practice in the European monarchy, reaching its peak during the reigns of Louis XIV, Louis XV, and Louis XVI, from the 1640s to 1790s. Even during the seventeenth and eighteenth centuries it was recognized that fashion was best shown on a body, even if it was on a lifeless mannequin.

This fashion doll is shown in Russian Court Dress of the early 19th century.
(Warwick Doll Museum. Copyright © Walter Scott, Bradford, England)

Designers Who Influenced Fashion Shows

Rose Bertin was the first dressmaker to be recognized by name. This French fashion creator was the dressmaker to Marie Antoinette, wife of Louis XVI. Dressmakers of the time would make up garments from a pattern, with fabric and trimming selected by the client. Despite her well known work for the queen, Rose Bertin achieved international fame with her fashion dolls that she sent to all the capitals of Europe to solicit orders. As a result of this international fame, Mademoiselle Bertin was given the nickname, *Minister of Fashion.*

The modern runway fashion show has its roots in the French Couture that began in the nineteenth century. Costume historians agree that Charles Frederick Worth, the English-born fashion innovator was the first couturier in France, opening his own Paris fashion house in 1858. Among Worth's revolutionary ideas was designing clothing for an individual woman, customizing the style, fabric and trimmings to the wearer. Made-to-order garments would be created for his clients from the samples in the salon. For his contributions in making the couture world nearly what it is today, Worth was given the nickname, *Father of Haute Couture.*

Worth had worked with fabrics and clothes in London before leaving for Paris in 1845. One of his first jobs in France was with Gagelin and Opigez, a retailer who sold fabrics, trimmings, coats, and shawls. It was the responsibility of the *demoiselle de magasin* (shopgirl) to show customers how the shawls looked on a living form *(Diehl, 1976, p 5).* Marie-Vernet, an original demoiselle de magasin, who later became Madame Worth, was perhaps the first fashion model when she showed shawls and the latest Worth creations to clients.

The House of Worth called the women who wore garments for clients to see how they looked on a living and moving person, **mannequins** *(Corinth, 1970, p 14)*. Up to this point, the term mannequin had previously referred to a stationary doll or dummy used as a display fixture. As Worth became more successful, he hired more young women to model at his *maison* or fashion house. These mannequins continued to show his collections to his customers.

Before the end of the century several other designers opened *Maisons de Haute Couture* in the manner of Charles Frederick Worth. These designers copied the promotional innovations of Worth and featured their designs on live models. By the 1920s French designers Paul Poiret, Madame Paquin, and Jean Patou made significant contributions to the development of the fashion show.

Paul Poiret known for liberating women from the corset, opened his couture house in 1904. This designer had a knack for promotion, among his contributions were his innovative and controversial window displays. Poiret also toured, making personal appearances, to show his fashions at chic resorts. Poiret even traveled to Russia with nine mannequins. He was one of the first couturiers to parade his mannequins at the races *(Diehl, 1976, p 6)*. Such events had a positive impact on his sales and image.

The House of **Paquin** was also known for parading models at the racetrack, but Paquin also staged such events at the opera. Paquin was the first designer to introduce the finale for her events. It is said that in one show 20 mannequins were dressed in white evening gowns as a tableau *(Diehl, 1976, p 7)*. This created a positive and lasting impression at the end of the show. Finales—exciting conclusions—have become universal and important to contemporary fashion shows.

It was common practice for couture houses to show their latest collections on a predetermined opening day. These dates were established by the Chambre Syndicale so that openings of the important designers would not conflict, enabling clients and the press to view several shows. After this premiere the show would be repeated twice each day for a month, with smaller shows for private clients. The ordinary dress rehearsal, which took place the

Models pose during a 1921 fashion show for the Wells Shop of Washington D.C. This early specialty store featured corsets, brassières, hats, and bonnets. (Reproduced from the Collections of the Library of Congress)

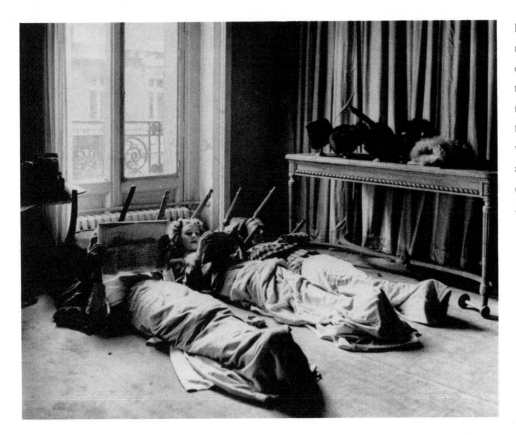

Lee Miller, a top *Vogue* model and World War II combat photographer, shot this photo of models relaxing before a Paris fashion show in 1945. It was one of the first shows after France was liberated. (Copyright © The Lee Miller Archives, 1992)

evening before the premiere, was held with the sales personnel and workers as the audience, giving the employees their only chance to see their labors.

Jean Patou primarily known for his contributions to sportswear and as a rival of Chanel, was associated with two important contributions to the fashion show—the press show and the use of American models in Paris. The press had been coming to report on the fashion collections since 1910. In 1921 Patou scheduled a special preview showing, the *repetition generale*, a full dress rehearsal for the influential representatives of the press, notable buyers and exceptional clients on an evening before his regular opening *(Etherington-Smith, 1983, pp 45-46)*. With the assistance of Elsa Maxwell, a popular party planner of the era and perhaps the first press agent, Patou converted the ordinary dress rehearsal into an extraordinary way to introduce the fashion season. The salon was festively decorated with flowers and spotlights. Guests were seated at tables with name cards and were treated to champagne, deluxe cigarettes and cigars, and sample bottles of Patou perfumes. The couturier Patou, his premier/premiere, head of the workroom, and his directrice/directeur, head of the salon, approved each model before she was allowed to show the garment to the audience. Since some fashion styles were rejected at this program, the audience observed the designer as he made his final eliminations from his collection. Patou's events led the way for the twice annual press shows held by the Paris couture throughout the twentieth century.

An American client complained that she had a hard time visualizing herself in the Patou clothing as it was shown on the French mannequins, whose figures were round compared to American figures. Patou traveled to America in 1924. With the assistance of Edna Woolman Chase, then editor of *Vogue* magazine, Elsie de Wolfe, decorator and interna-

Private clients and influential members of the press were always anxious to view the latest Chanel collections. The audience views Chanel's fashion show in 1959. (Marc Riboud/Magnum Photos)

tional socialite, **Edward Steichen**, photographer, and **Condé Nast**, publisher of *Vogue*, Patou selected six American models—Lillian Farley, Josephine Armstrong, Dorothy Raynor, Caroline Putnam, Edwina Prue, and Rosalind Stair—to return with him to Paris. Although Patou had originally planned on hiring three models, he doubled the number selected due to the favorable impression they created. The young women "of refined manner" gave prestige to the profession of modeling. They were paid $40 per week and given the opportunity to purchase ensembles from Patou for as little as $25 *(Etherington-Smith, 1983, p 82)*. The use of American models changed the ideal of international physical beauty to the thinner and more athletic shapes that these American women possessed.

Paquin's contribution to the fashion show was the finale, but it was Patou who influenced the dramatic opening. For his spring 1925 presentation, he had French and American models make their first entrance in a single file parade wearing the toile—the simple robe worn between fittings in the dressing room. He demonstrated that the physical form was the same regardless of nationality and served as the inspiration for his designs. The audience was entertained and were preconditioned to like the collection *(Etherington-Smith, 1983, p 45)*.

Fashion shows remained as fashion parades through the thirties, forties, and fifties. The quality of these fashion productions improved as did the technology in this time period. Many of these shows rivaled Broadway musicals with stage sets, lighting, music, and fabulous mannequins. This basic format remained consistent until the sixties.

The creativity and energy of the swinging 1960s led to major changes in fashion and the way it was presented. British designer **Mary Quant** was at the forefront of these changes. Certain models were known for their work in the photographic media while other models worked the runway shows. However, Quant felt that photographic models rather than runway models knew how to move around in clothes, so she selected nine of them to dance down the stairs and runway at her shop, Knightsbridge Bazaar. Since this era models have worked each field interchangeably.

Quant's staging, use of innovative props, and dancing led to more active fashion shows.

Contemporary jazz music was taped for an uninterrupted pace. The show consisted of 40 garments and was shown in 14 minutes. One outfit featured a model wearing a Norfolk jacket and knickers and carrying a shotgun and a dead pheasant for a hunting scene. Models wearing party dresses carried oversized champagne glasses. Absolutely no commentary was spoken *(Quant, 1966, pp 94-95)*. This period marked the elimination of commentary from press and trade shows.

Thêâtre de la Mode

A fashion show presentation unique to the twentieth century took place at the end of World War II. Paris designers in a liberated France wanted to let the world know that they were ready to resume fashion leadership despite limited resources. Unable to launch a full scale fashion exhibition, designers, artists, and musicians collaborated to present Thêâtre de la Mode, allowing the world to see the French spring-summer collection of 1946, the first to be designed for export since the war. Petits mannequins, or fashion dolls first used in the fourteenth century, were revived for this exhibition. Although the presentation did not use live models it did present fashion on the human form in the style of a spectacular fashion show.

This project was coordinated through the Chambre Syndicale de la Haute Couture Parisienne. It brought together designers who otherwise would have concealed their work from competitors *(Train, 1991, p 65)*.

An exhibit of 228 petits mannequins featured the latest work of the French designers. The mannequins were presented in 12 theatrical sets to provide the proper environment for morning, afternoon or evening attire. Participating couture houses agreed to create from one to five outfits for display.

Susan Train prepares a fashion doll for presentation in Thêâtre de la Mode. The doll is dressed in a day suit by O'Rossen complete with suede gloves by Hermes.
(Jean Luca Hure/NYT Pictures)

Vogue magazine sponsored the first doll fashion show in America in 1896. This was one of the first benefit fashion shows, raising $500 at the opening.

(Copyright © 1896 by The Fashion Company, Courtesy of *Vogue* Magazine, The Condé Nast Publications Inc.)

Model Doll Show

UNDER THE MANAGEMENT OF VOGUE

IN AID OF

THE SCARLET FEVER AND DIPHTHERIA HOSPITAL

SHERRY'S, MARCH 20TH, 21ST AND 23D

THE Show will be opened with a Private View, Friday, 20 March, at 3 o'clock, and continue on Saturday, 21 March, and Monday 23 March. The extraordinary feature will be dolls dressed as models of special costumes and of prevailing fashions. These dolls will be dressed by the leading designers of New York, and present a great variety of subject and treatment.

TICKETS - - - FIFTY CENTS

PATRONESSES :

Mrs. Charles B. Alexander	Mrs. Richard H. Derby	Mrs. Eugene Kelly	Mrs. C. Albert Stevens
Miss Malvina Appleton	Mrs. Arthur M. Dodge	Mrs. Edward King	Mrs. William Rhinelander Sr
Mrs. John Jacob Astor	Mrs. Cleveland H. Dodge	Mrs. Gustav Kissel	Mrs. Joseph Stickney
Mrs. Charles T. Barney	Mrs. John R. Drexel	Mrs. Luther Kountze	Mrs. T. Suffern Tailer
Miss de Barril	Mrs. Nicholas Fish	Mrs. Charles Lanier	Mrs. Henry A. C. Taylor
Mrs. Edmund L. Baylies	Miss de Forest	Mrs. J. Lawrence Lee	Mrs. Jonathan Thorne
Mrs. August Belmont	Mrs. George B. de Forest	Mrs. Edward A. Le Roy, Jr.	Mrs. Henry Graff Trevor
Mrs. David Wolfe Bishop	Miss Furniss	Mrs. Charles H. Marshall	Mrs. John B. Trevor
Mrs. Heber R. Bishop	Mrs. John Lyon Gardiner	Mrs. Ogden Mills	Mrs. Paul Tuckerman
Mrs. William T. Blodgett	Mrs. Elbridge T. Gerry	Mrs. John W. Minturn	Mrs. Arthur Turnure
Mrs. James A. Burden	Mrs. G. G. Haven	Mrs. Trenor L. Park	Mrs. Cornelius Vanderbilt
Miss Callender	Mrs. Peter Cooper Hewitt	Mrs. James W. Pinchot	Mrs. F. W. Vanderbilt
Mrs. A. Cass Canfield	Mrs. Thomas Hitchcock	Mrs. George B. Post	Mrs. William Seward Webb
Mrs. Henry E. Coe	Mrs. G. G. Howland	Mrs. M. Taylor Pyne	Mrs. Geo. Peabody Wetmore
Mrs. Joseph H. Choate	Mrs. Edward W. Humphreys	Mrs. Jules Reynal	Mrs. John C. Wilmerding
Mrs. H. H. Curtis	Mrs. Morris K. Jesup	Mrs. T. J. Oakley Rhinelander	Mrs. Orme Wilson
Mrs. Brockholst Cutting	Mrs. William Jay	Mrs. Sidney Dillon Ripley	Mrs. Buchanan Winthrop
Miss Cuyler	Mrs. Walter Jennings	Mrs. Henry Sloane	Mrs. Frank Spencer Witherbee
Mrs. Francis Delafield	Mrs. Frederic R. Jones	Mrs. William Douglas Sloane	

Further particulars, if desired, will be supplied by the management, VOGUE, 154 FIFTH AVENUE, NEW YORK.

vi

The 27.5 inch wire figurines were built from sketches developed by Eliane Bonabel. Plaster heads constructed by sculptor Joan Rebull were added to the figures so that they could have real coiffures and hats.

The art director for the project was Christian (Bebé) Bérard, a Parisian artist. He called upon his friends in the arts, theater, and literary world to participate. Balenciaga, Hermés, Balmain, Lanvin, Molyneux, Schiaparelli, Worth, and Ricci were among the fashion designers who participated.

The show was originally produced to raise money to help war victims. The exhibition traveled to England, Spain, Denmark, Sweden, and Austria. The following year the show was sent to New York and San Francisco with updated fashions. With limited resources the show's sponsors could not afford to return the mannequins and clothing to Paris. The display was forgotten and it was assumed that the doll collection was lost until it was discovered at the *Maryhill Museum of Art* in Goldendale, Washington in 1983. The garments and accessories were returned to Paris for restoration in 1987. An exhibit featuring 171 dolls opened at the *Musée des Arts de la Mode* in Paris in 1990. The exhibit moved to the *Costume Institute of The Metropolitan Museum of Art*, New York, later that year. The exhibit will be permanently located at the Maryhill Museum of Art.

Associations that Influenced Fashion Shows

The American ready-to-wear industry was taking shape in the early years of the twentieth century, and American manufacturers used live models to present the latest collections at the major regional trade marts. The most important trade shows were held in Chicago and New York.

The "Merchandise Buyers Exposition and Fashion Show at the New Grand Central Palace" held in 1912 in New York staged two live fashion parades daily. While a local orchestra played the popular songs of the day, live models walked across a stage carrying cards with simply the manufacturer's name indicated. No evidence of commentary was reported at this time *(Diehl, 1976, p 7)*.

In 1914, the Chicago Garment Manufacturers Association presented an elaborate fashion show to the 5,000 people attending this market. One hundred mannequins showed 250 garments in nine scenes. The rehearsal was filmed and distributed to local theaters across the United States. This show used a stage and a large platform or runway to bring the clothing closer to the audience. This was perhaps the first use of a fashion show "runway" *(Corinth, 1970, pp 16-17)*.

Edna Woolman Chase, editor of *Vogue* magazine, combined several elements, including trade shows, society leaders, and a charitable benefit for a wartime cause into the first major fashion show for the public. On November 4, 1914, the "Fashion Fête" was produced featuring American designs at the time that Paris was threatened by World War I. The show was held as a benefit for widows and orphans of the allied countries.

With the assistance and patronage of the society women of the day, *Vogue* presented fashions at a gala event held at the Ritz-Carlton hotel. Clothing from Henri Bendel, a fashion leader of the time, was selected by a committee of seven society women as well as Mrs. Chase and Helen Koues also from *Vogue*. The evening started with dinner; it was followed by a fashion show and later dancing. The show was repeated for two days in the afternoons and evenings.

Vogue advertised for models for the Fashion Fête. At this time no formal schools existed for models, and dressmaker models although an integral part of French couture were employed by only a few New York dressmakers. The applicants were rehearsed by *Vogue* and instructed on how to walk, pivot and show the garments. The following year, partly because of the influence of the first Fête, mannequins as models started to become an important factor to the American fashion scene *(Chase, 1954, pp 124-127)*. The use of the fashion show to raise money for philanthropic organizations has been common throughout the twentieth century.

By the 1920s fashion shows were an accepted form of introducing new lines of apparel to the fashion press, retailers, and consumers. Fashion shows were no longer a novelty, they were professionally staged events that people looked forward to.

In 1914 Edna Woolman Chase, editor of *Vogue*, decided to feature American designers in the "Fashion Fête."
(Copyright © 1914 by The *Vogue* Company. Courtesy of *Vogue* Magazine, The Condé Nast Publications Inc.)

A flare of footlights, a moment of silence, the curtains part, and—America passes judgment on what America can do

The group that helped to set high standards for professionalism in the production of fashion shows was the Fashion Group. The Fashion Group was founded in 1931 by 75 women fashion executives. One of the purposes of the group then, as it is now, is to provide a central source of information on fashion trends. Fashion shows for members and guests were presented almost from the beginning of the organization. The first "Fashion Futures" event was held on September 11, 1935. It was described as the first, un-propaganda, un-commercialized and un-subsidized fashion show ever presented *(Corinth, 1970, p 21)*.

By 1992 The Fashion Group International, Inc. had more than 6,000 members in 45 regional groups *(The Fashion Group Membership Directory, 1992)*. Members can be found in the United States, Canada, England, France, Mexico, Korea, Japan, South Africa, and South America. Membership is made up of women with executive status, representing the fields of fashion, cosmetics, and the home.

Various volunteer committees provide unique programs. Two of the most important international programs are the slide presentations of seasonal fashion trends and the only live presentation of the European Haute Couture Collections in America. The programs and Trend Reports are available to all members and regional groups.

Regional groups take on fashion leadership in the various markets. For example the International Fashion Group of Dallas, Inc. sponsors an annual "Career Day" for students of fashion merchandising and design. The day concludes with a fashion show featuring apparel and accessories created by fashion design students. The show is professionally produced by the Kim Dawson Agency—the fashion show production and modeling agency affiliated with the Dallas Apparel Mart. The show serves as a design competition with trips to Paris and scholarships as the awards.

EUROPEAN FASHION SHOWS

London, Paris, and Milan are the major European cities where fashion trends are presented, analyzed, purchased for international trade, and worn. More than 50,000 fashion professionals and fashion followers visit these European fashion capitals twice each year to view dazzling fashion presentations. During February/March the fall ready-to-wear collections are featured. The spring lines are introduced in September/October.

French Couture Fashion Shows

Haute couture is the French high fashion industry featuring clothing produced for a client's individual measurements. Couture shows are the source of fashion leadership and innovation that supports the trickle-down theory of fashion adoption. They are held in January and July each year. Items are first presented at higher prices to a limited audience and later are adopted at lower prices by a larger audience. These innovations serve as inspiration for mainstream fashion houses. For example in the 1980s the "pouf skirts" created by Christian Lacroix for the House of Patou led to a variety of mass market adaptations. In the U.S. junior market, consumers wore skirts with layers of ruffles that imitated the "poufs" from Lacroix.

The peak of fashion showmanship is displayed twice yearly at couture openings This model (left) appears on the runway in an original French design. Backstage at Karl Lagerfeld's ready-to-wear show held in France (right). (Both photos: *WWD*)

Most French couture houses are laid out in a similar manner. The first floor contains the ready-to-wear boutique that features apparel, accessories, and perfume. The second floor consists of the Salon, fitting rooms, and offices. The Salon is the area where garments and accessories are presented to clients. The *directrice* is in charge of the Salon. Models quickly enter the room carrying cards with the garment number. Absolutely no commentary is used during this presentation. The upper floors of the building accommodate the *ateliers* (work-rooms) where the *midinettes* (seamstresses) work. The public is not admitted to the work-rooms due to the secrecy of the couture designs.

Chambre Syndicale de la Couture Parisienne There are 24 creators recognized as members of the **Chambre Syndicale de la Couture Parisienne**, the trade organization of the Paris couture. In order to be recognized as a member of the haute couture the company must meet the following qualifications:

1. A formal written request, with the sponsorship of two current members is presented to and voted on by the entire organization.
2. Workrooms, providing quality workmanship, must be established in Paris.
3. Collections are designed by the designer or an employee of the house. Garments are individually made to a client's measurements.
4. Collections must be presented twice annually in January and July during the times set by the Chambre Syndicale.
5. At least 75 designs must be included in the collection.
6. The house must have three models employed throughout the year.
7. The house must employ a minimum of 20 sewing workers in the workrooms.

Many of the major couture houses take their collections to other countries after the Paris shows. Some of the most important looks are flown to New York, Tokyo, and the Middle East and shown to potential customers.

Galeries Lafayette, an internationally known French department store, produces weekly fashion shows for foreign tourists. These examples of advertising materials include a press release, shopping bags, and invitations promoting Galeries Lafayette consumer shows.

```
                    1992 FASHION SHOWS

1 - WEEKLY FASHION SHOWS

        - Free show at 11 a.m throughout the year.
        - A drink and snacks will be served during the show.
        - Individuals as well as small groups -- Reservations
        mandatory.


        FASHION SHOWS EVERY WEDNESDAY AT 11:00 AM THROUGHOUT THE
        YEAR, AND EVERY WEDNESDAY AND FRIDAY AT 11:00 AM FROM MARCH
        THROUGH OCTOBER.

3 - TAILOR MADE FASHION SHOWS

        - A show can be arranged for your groups any day Monday
        through Saturday, throughout the year.
        - The show may be accompanied by any number of options from
        a luncheon to a champagne cocktail.
        - The base price for the show is 12.000 FF (+18.6% VAT).
        - Inquire for menus and food service prices at the address
        or phone number below.
        - Special decoration is possible; audio material is at your
        disposal for shows at our store.
        - A 25% deposit will be requested upon booking. In case of
        cancellation less than 15 days before the scheduled show,
        your deposit will not be refunded.

FOR ALL THESE FASHION SHOWS

- Your customers will find a warm welcome and comfortable seating
arrangements in our private "Opéra Salon", 7th floor of the main
building, direct access.

- Five models and 45 outfits signed by the world's leading
fashion designers dazzle the spectators.

- A multilingual commentary and audio-visual presentation
accompany the models.

- We can organize shows at the location of your choice
(Prestigious Parisian hotels, Seine river boats etc...)

                    GALERIES LAFAYETTE
                      Milena JOVOVIC
            40, Blvd Haussmann 75009 Paris France

        Phone: (33.1) 48 74 02 30, (33.1) 42 82 30 25
        Telex: 280 357 GALFA - FAX (33.1) 40.16.09.15
```

French Ready-to-Wear Shows

The **prêt-à-porter** is the ready-to-wear fashion industry in Paris. The **defiles des createurs** are the designer runway shows featuring the newest creations from French as well as by Italian, Japanese, American, and other international designers. The circus-like atmosphere of these wildly exotic presentations results in a festive and inspirational event. Designers send invitations to buyers, the press, and clients, but the crush for seats shows evidence of the many gate crashers.

The ready-to-wear shows are scheduled by the **Fédération Française du prêt-à-porter Feminin.** Paris fashion shows have been presented at a variety of locations such as tents in the Tuileries, the Bois de Boulogne, the Palais de Congres, and the Louvre. The Porte de Versailles, a former railway station, is the location of an exhibition/trade fair featuring the, "International Ladies' Ready-to-Wear and Boutique Clothing Exhibition." Over 1,500 apparel and accessory firms show their lines in booths. Firms are grouped by theme or country. Participants attend mini-fashion shows or a major runway presentation.

French Retail Shows

The two largest department stores in Paris are *Printemps* and *Galeries Lafayette*. Both of these giant retailers regularly produce fashion shows for their clients. At Galeries Lafayette a special weekly or twice weekly fashion show is presented for their international visitors. Over 10,000 people viewed the show created for the non-Parisian audience in 1989.

A staff of about 40 people are involved in the production of the Galeries Lafayette "International Fashion Show." This crew includes models, dressers, technicians, hostesses, and the commentator. The show was created in 1987 to entertain visiting dignitaries and attract foreign visitors to Galeries Lafayette. Approximately 150 people attend each show which is promoted using brochures and advertising on airlines and in hotels as well as through the French tourism industry.

All visitors make reservations, letting the store know what nationalities to expect at any given show. The commentator then adjusts the commentary to fit the languages necessary for the audience at that performance. French, Japanese, Spanish, Italian, and English are the most common languages spoken, but other translations may be accommodated.

The show is divided into scenes with an audio-visual presentation used to highlight Paris and emphasize the various themes. Milena Jovonic of Galeries Lafayette, Paris, reported that the show consisted of six different scenes:
  1. Lingerie—pajamas, robes, bustiers
  2. Avant Premiere—very young trend-setting fashions
  3. Couturiere—exclusive designer and classic fashions
  4. Cocktail—short evening wear
  5. Dinner—long dresses
  6. Wedding—finale with wedding apparel

The producers do not attempt to change the clothing each week to meet newly arriving merchandise. The show is formulated to emphasize "looks and tendencies" rather than specific garments. Clothing and accessories are changed four times each year, with new items added regularly to freshen the show in between major seasonal changes.

Italian Fashion Shows

The Italian couture is governed by the Camera Nationale della Alta Moda Italia. This organization oversees the activities of the couture designers and ready-to-wear, shoe, and accessory manufacturers. The Camera provides organization for the group events including the couture shows in Rome and the ready-to-wear shows in Milan. The Italian couture has declined in importance while the ready-to-wear industry has been gaining in international significance. Much of the high fashion industry and design activities take place in Rome.

However, due to the aggressive nature of the Paris couture, many of the Italian couture designers are showing their collections in Paris instead of Rome.

The semi-annual fashion shows featuring Italian ready-to-wear are held in Milan just prior to the designer shows in Paris. Primarily known for its knitwear, sportswear and accessories by such creators as Giorgio Armani, Missoni, Fendi, and Valentino, Milan is aggressively promoting itself as the fashion center of Italy. The fast-paced Milan ready-to-wear shows are presented at the *Fiera*, a three-story convention center located on the outskirts of Milan.

Laura Biagiotti is typical of the Italian ready-to-wear producers. Mrs. Biagiotti lives and designs in Rome. Her international showroom and sales force are located in Milan. She shows only two collections each year. The collections are put together in Rome but they are shown in Milan. A complete collection may consist of as many as 500 pieces. During the 35- to 40-minute show approximately 160 pieces, representative of her total collection, are shown on 35 to 40 models.

British Fashion Shows

London, the city associated with the 1960s fashion revolution of Mary Quant, Carnaby Street, and the Mod Look, remains as the center of innovative and classic British fashion. The few remaining couture designers cater to the British royalty and have limited influence on international fashion. The two main fashion presentations are the London Designer Collections and the British Designer Shows. Designers Zandra Rhodes, Bruce Oldfield, Caroline Charles, and Jean Muir along with Wendy Dagworthy and Betty Jackson lead the talented British designers. Young experimental designers continue to spark interest in London as a fashion center. The royal family takes an active interest in London Fashion Week. The Princess of Wales, Lady Diana, has shown attention and support for the industry and participated in the opening ceremonies of the twice annual trade fair.

In the 1990s, fashion shows are a routine part of doing business in all segments of the fashion industry. Understanding the development of the fashion show may enhance the enthusiasm for producing fashion shows. Innovations in sound and lighting, multi-media events using slides, film and video offer greater opportunities to present exciting fashion presentations. These specialized fashion presentations are a routine part of doing business in the fashion industry all over the world.

KEY FASHION SHOW TERMS

cooperative advertising	haute couture	sales promotion
defiles des createurs	mannequins	secondary resources
directrice / directeur	national promotion	trade promotion
fashion dolls	premier / premiere	tertiary resources
Fashion Fête	prêt-à-porter	trickle-down theory
fashion parade	primary resources	
fashion show	retail promotion	

Key People Who Influenced the Fashion Show

Rose Bertin	Jean Patou	Elsie de Wolfe
Edna Woolman Chase	Paul Poiret	Charles Frederick Worth
Elsa Maxwell	Mary Quant	
House of Paquin	Edward Steichen	

ADDITIONAL READINGS

1. Corinth, *Fashion Showmanship* (1970): Show Business in the Fashion World (Chapter 1) and The History of Fashion Shows (Chapter 2).

2. Diehl, *How to Produce a Fashion Show* (1976): History of Fashion Shows (Chapter 1) and Why to Have a Fashion Show (Chapter 2).

3. Guerin, *Creative Fashion Presentations* (1987): Europe: A Fashion Parade Extraordinaire (Chapter 8).

4. For profiles on historical and contemporary fashion designers see Stegemeyer, *Who's Who in Fashion*, 2nd ed (text, 1988 and supplement, 1992) and *McDowell, McDowell's Directory of Twentieth Century Fashion* (1987).

5. See the following for more comprehensive information on individual biographies of designers: Etherington-Smith, *Patou* (1983); Madsen, *Chanel: A Woman of Her Own* (1990); Moor, J. *Perry Ellis* (1988); Quant, *Quant by Quant* (1966); Chase, *Always in Vogue* (1954); White, *Poiret* (1973).

6. A more complete discussion of the Thêàtre de la Mode can be found by Train, *Thêàtre de la Mode* (1991).

2

Types of Fashion Shows

Since fashion shows are staged to sell a variety of products at various levels of marketing distribution channels, shows take on various forms dependent upon the desired outcome of the individual, business, or group sponsoring the event. It is important to consider the various types of fashion shows. They can be very small informal activities with limited preparation and casual execution or spectacular events with months of preparation involving a large number of people.

FASHION SHOW CATEGORIES

Fashion shows are defined by four different production styles or categories. These include the:
• Production Show   • Formal Runway Show   • Informal Show   • Video Production

The Production Show

The most elaborate and expensive fashion show is the production show. This type of event is the most dramatic or theatrical, and may also be called a dramatized or spectacular show. Fashion trends are emphasized using special entertainment, backdrops or scenery, lighting effects, live or specially produced music, and perhaps dancing or specialized choreography. The production show is generally at least one hour in length. As few as 15 models or as many as 50 models may be used to emphasize the trends depending upon the needs of the sponsoring group.

The production show requires a great deal of organization and advance planning. Normally a show of this caliber would include some form of hospitality such as a luncheon, dinner, or hors d'oeuvres and cocktails. It may be keyed to a special event such as a fund-raiser for a local charity. The *Geoffrey Beene Collections*, presented for the *Arizona Heart Institute Foundation*

Delegates to the 1992 Democratic National Convention in New York City were treated to more than political activities. Seventh Avenue designers displayed their latest lines on a 120-foot runway under a tent in Central Park. (*WWD*)

Figure 2-1

Fashion Show Categories

Type	Style	Merchandise
Production	Dramatized Spectacular	Couture Evening Bridal Ready-to-Wear
Formal Runway	Fashion Parade	Seasonal Trends Specialty Markets Ready-to-Wear
Informal	Tea Room Trunk Show Hatbox Mannequin Modeling	All Types of Merchandise
Video	Point-of-Purchase Instructional Documentary	All Types of Merchandise

in Phoenix, Arizona is an example of this dramatic show type. Another example is *The Symphony Fashion Gala*, a cooperative production of Horne's Department Store and the *Pittsburgh Symphony Association*. This annual event is staged to raise funds for the Pittsburgh Symphony Orchestra. The production show is often presented to large groups such as the standing room only audience of nearly 3,000 that attend the Pittsburgh event.

The Formal Runway Show

The formal runway show is a conventional presentation of fashion that is similar to a parade. In fact, this kind of fashion show may also be called a fashion parade. The length of the show is generally 30 minutes to one hour and features a series of models who walk or dance on a runway in a sequential manner. Models may walk down the runway alone, in pairs or in groups. The main characteristic is the use of a runway and models coming out one after another. This type of show requires advance planning and organization for a professional appearance and involves all of the following fashion show elements:

- Theme (merchandise and scene development)
- Special location (auditorium, hotel or restaurant, sales floor)
- Staging and lighting
- Models
- Music (live or sound system)
- Commentary (if appropriate)

A formal runway show may be directed toward a specific consumer or a specialty market such as career women, college students or children. It may also serve as the forum for a seasonal promotion showing several important color, fabric or silhouette trends at that particular time period. Some form of hospitality such as a dinner, lunch, or light refreshments, may also be expected.

A formal runway show (left) features single models or groups of models on a runway. This traditional type of show may also be called a parade. Informal shows (right) give audiences a chance to see models stroll around showrooms, restaurants, or other intimate settings. (*WWD*)

The Informal Fashion Show

A casual presentation of garments and accessories on models is an informal fashion show. In this type of fashion show no theatrical elements such as music, lighting or runway are used. While there are no special staging requirements for informal fashion shows, props may be used to enhance the image of the garments being featured. Selling is simply left to the model who walks through the store sales floor, manufacturer's showroom, or restaurant. This type of fashion show requires very little preparation compared to the production and formal runway shows.

The sponsoring group hires models for a day-rate. The models simply walk around the predetermined area often carrying a sign, business card, or handout with information about the merchandise, department, or store where the merchandise is located.

Restaurants might choose to feature fashions from a local retail store on a regular basis. This type of informal fashion show has been referred to as tea-room modeling. The store selects three to five models, perhaps store employees. These models are fitted into outfits prior to the show. During the show the models walk from table to table showing what they are wearing. Models regularly carry business or discount cards from the store to leave with the audience. Models should be careful to not interrupt or disturb the customers of the restaurant.

Informal modeling in a store may take place in a specific department or throughout the entire store. Usually an assistant fashion coordinator will handle scheduling models and select garments in cooperation with the buyer or department manager. The fashion coordinator will also work with accessories personnel to achieve a total look and project the desired fashion statement.

During market weeks, held to present new seasonal items to the trade, the manufacturer's showroom manager may hire models to wear the new line and walk around the showroom.

Retail buyers may not be able to see a formal fashion show presented to the trade, but they may wish to see how certain garments from the line look on the human form. Models will be able to show these garments in an informal manner, putting on sample garments as desired by retail buyers and showroom personnel.

Trunk Show A specific type of informal fashion show that features garments from one manufacturer or designer at a retail store is a trunk show. The complete line from the manufacturer or designer is shipped to a store in "trunks" or sales representative's cases. The manufacturer or designer sends a representative of their company to interact with the customers during the in-store event. Models walk through the retail store, emphasizing the garments.

There are several advantages for the manufacturer and the retailer in conducting trunk shows. Retailers rarely buy entire collections from a particular manufacturer for their stores. Normally, retail stores edit from the manufacturer's offerings, buying only the colors and styles they feel will sell to their customers. With a trunk show, customers are able to see complete collections from the producer. They are able to order any styles, sizes or colors they like in the line. Retailers benefit by selling merchandise without taking the risk of carrying that merchandise in the permanent stock.

Another advantage for the manufacturer as well as the retailer is being able to evaluate consumer reaction to the line, learning customers' preferences and best sellers. At a personal appearance at I. Magnin, designer Calvin Klein took the opportunity to spend time with his clients and discuss their specific needs for the following season. The designer could incorporate the customers' desires into the next collection through this type of interaction. Personal appearances enhance the retailer's image. Customers enjoy meeting a celebrity and being able to ask questions about the garments. Any unique features about the products are discussed. Customers learn how to wear styles and accessories. Calvin Klein's appearance resulted in $250,000 in sales for two days.

Hatbox Show The hatbox show requires a small area and a limited budget. In this type of show a single person acts as a model and commentator. The individual presents the show by modeling an outfit, then changes into another outfit behind a screen, while at the same time maintaining the commentary.

The model/commentator for this type of show must have an extensive fashion vocabulary, must be able to ad lib, and feel extremely comfortable with his/her fashion knowledge. The success of this type of show is dependent upon the abilities of the "personality" staging the show.

Mannequin Modeling Some retail stores, shopping centers, and fashion exhibits at fairs have utilized this simple form of the fashion show. Mannequin modeling involves live models in a store window or on a display platform. These live models strike poses like the stationary display props they have been named after. This type of informal modeling requires a lot of discipline and composure by the models who pose in stiff positions. Inevitably customers try to make these models laugh and move.

Video Productions

Throughout history the fashion industry has always had a fascination with the latest technology. The fashion industry has aggressively adopted video technology in presenting fashion at both the wholesale and retail levels. One of the first uses of video production was at the designer/manufacturer level. Nearly every designer and manufacturer would videotape their runway shows. These tapes would be used to train the national sales force or given to retailers to show in their stores where customers could stop and view these presentations. The videotape would become a silent salesperson. The consumer was able to view how the designer/manufacturer envisioned the total look of the merchandise. Models are often selected based on their video appeal.

Now there are several types of video productions used. These include the **point-of-purchase**, **instructional**, and **documentary videos**. The point-of-purchase video is placed right on the sales floor of a retail store. Consumers are given the opportunity to see the original manufacturer's runway show or an action view of how to wear the merchandise. Instructional videos are created for in-store training of sales personnel, and may also be presented to the store's customers. They show the current information on fashion trends in addition to the special features of the products. The documentary video focuses on the designer or behind-the-scenes activities of the manufacturer. These may be used for training company employees, produced for television shows or used at a retail store for point-of-purchase entertainment.

Contemporary fashion show videos take their cue from the music and electronic media. These videos combine all of the theatrical elements from the entertainment industry. The modern consumer has grown up with television and expects a highly sophisticated video presentation.

SPECIALIZED FASHION PRESENTATIONS

Fashion shows may be differentiated by various characteristics such as market level within the industry (primary, secondary, tertiary resources), the type and price of merchandise, audience, production style and size, type of model, and where the show is held.

Historically, fashion shows produced within the United States have developed into specialized fashion presentations aimed at certain segments within the industry. These specialized fashion presentations include the:

- Trade show
- Apparel mart show

- Trade association show
- Press show

They are designed to show new fashions produced by manufacturers to retail buyers. Other specialized fashion presentations are produced by retailers to show new merchandise to store personnel or consumers. These shows include: *in-store training, specialty market shows, new store openings, magazine tie-ins, cooperative fashion shows, home sewing fashion shows, benefit shows,* and *regional or cultural shows.*

The Trade Show

The term **trade** refers to any activity aimed at distribution of fashion and related products within the industry. Trade shows, also called **industrial shows**, are produced to sell raw materials to manufacturers or manufactured goods to retailers.

Fashion shows presented by fiber/fabric producers are aimed at apparel designers, piece-goods buyers for apparel producers, retailers, and members of the press. The primary objective of this type of show is to illustrate the benefits of the raw material to the design and manufacture of the fashion product.

Apparel manufacturers or designers offer their products to potential retail buyers and members of the press. The objective of this type of fashion program is to sell their interpretation of fashion trends to potential customers. Collections are differentiated from those offered by other companies based on innovation, superiority, and value to the ultimate consumer. These shows are generally staged as productions or fashion parades.

One of the advantages of trade shows is that it is possible for retailers and the press to view a large number of manufacturers in one location. Trade shows may be held from one to four times each year. Some shows are exclusive to one product line such as Ski Industry America held in Las Vegas, Nevada, annually. Other trade shows such as the International Fashion and Boutique Show may involve several categories of merchandise.

The cost to manufacturers to participate in trade shows differs with the various organizations. A flat fee may be required by some groups. Or a fee plus a space charge depending upon the size of the space required by other groups. Some shows are more exclusive, demanding screening by a review panel.

There are five major categories of trade shows. These include fibers and fabrics, women's, men's, and children's apparel, and accessories. *International Fabric Exhibition* and *Yarn Fair* are examples of trade shows held in the fabrics and fibers classification. *American Designers at the Drake*, *Donna Moda*, and *Special Size Show* are examples of women's apparel trade shows. Men's apparel trade shows are represented by *Designer's Collective, NAMSB (National Association of Men's Sportswear Designers)*, and *Uomo Moda*. The children's apparel trade show is *International Kids Fashion Show*. Accessories are the featured product line at the following trade shows: *Accessorie Circuit, FAE (Fashion Accessories Expo)*, and *National Fashion Jewelry Accessory Showcase*.

Albert Nipon speaks with a customer in the retail store after a show highlighting his merchandise. Customers enjoy meeting such celebrities at special designer events.

Fashion designers often promote products beyond apparel. With cooperation from Dillard's, Bob Mackie made a special appearance to launch his fragrance "Mackie".

Manufacturer's Fashion Show The most common type of trade show is the **manufacturer's fashion show**. This type of show may be held in the manufacturer's showroom or at some outside location such as a hotel or restaurant. The purpose of the manufacturer's show is to introduce the new line to retail buyers and the media. The manufacturer's show is presented during market week. Market week is the time designated for producers of a specific category of merchandise to open sales on the season's new styles.

Market weeks for women's apparel are generally held five times each year. These seasons include: fall, holiday, resort, spring, and summer. The presentation of this type of show is held approximately two to six months prior to the time merchandise will arrive in the retail stores. Shows are held that far in advance to allow the manufacturer ample time to produce the merchandise to meet the demands of the retail selling season.

Designer Show Designer shows are ready-to-wear manufacturer's shows that feature a well-known designer. The **designer show** features the work of the creator whose name the company takes. Typically 75 to 100 garments are presented in about 30 minutes.

Despite all of the preparations the designer or manufacturer trade show is a one-time event. Unlike the theatrical productions on Broadway in New York there usually are no repeat performances of trade shows. These shows are often videotaped to be distributed to the national sales force or retail organizations.

The Apparel Mart Show

Regional **apparel marts** are wholesale centers located in major cities throughout the United States. Marts lease space to manufacturers who are able to offer their lines closer to the retailer's geographic location so that retail buyers do not have to travel to New York City to purchase merchandise. These fashion centers offer the convenience of many manufacturers in one location.

Figure 2-2

Show Type Characteristics

	Couture	Trade	Consumer
Audience	Private clients	Private clients	Customers of the
	Major retailers	Major retailers	retailer or manufacturer
	Press	Press	Press
Merchandise	Custom Made	Ready-to-Wear	Ready-to-Wear
	Clothing	Designer	Wearable Art
		Mass Production	
Prices	Prestige	High	High
		Moderate	Moderate
			Mass
Production	Production Show	Production Show	Production Show
	Formal Runway	Formal Runway	Formal Runway
	Video Show	Video Show	Informal Show
			Trunk Show
			Hatbox Show
			Mannequin Modeling
			Video Show
Size	Large	Medium	Small
		Large	Medium
			Large
Models	Professional	Professional	Professional or Amateur
Location	Paris	Major Market	Any town or city
	Milan	Hotels	Store sales floor
	London	Showrooms	Hotels
	New York	Market Centers	Restaurants
		Rooms	Schools
		Museums	Theaters
			Local Museums

Many small store buyers have found the regional centers to be very responsive to their needs. In addition to the convenience and reduced expenses, the regional marts sponsor retailing seminars and fashion shows for participants.

The major apparel marts are located in Los Angeles, Dallas, Chicago, and Atlanta. Other regional market centers include the Miami International Merchandise Mart, Denver Merchandise Mart, Carolina Trade Mart in Charlotte, North Carolina, San Francisco Mart, Northeast Trade Center in Woburn, Massachusetts, Radisson Center in Minneapolis, and Trade Center in Kansas City, Missouri. These centers make vendors accessible for many small retailers who find it difficult to visit the major market centers. The convenience and generally lower cost associated with visiting a regional center are adding to their popularity.

Regional apparel marts introduce the new lines of merchandise through fashion trend shows held for the retail buyers at the start of a market week. According to Yvette Crosby, former fashion director for the California Apparel Mart, she had approximately 48 hours to pull together a fashion show for the center. This involved selecting merchandise to be shown from the various showrooms, coordinating into scenes the diverse themes of goods being presented, hiring and training the models, and staging the show in the apparel mart theater. Although it was hectic, the show was pulled together at the last minute. Commentary was not used. Music was selected and taped to coordinate with the looks being featured. Dramatic lighting emphasized the changes in groups or themes.

At apparel mart fashion shows fashion buyers are given an opportunity to sort the themes being presented by the manufacturers prior to visiting individual showrooms. These fashion trend shows help the retailers pinpoint the merchandise and trends that would meet the needs of their particular customers. These shows are an entertaining and uplifting start to the chaotic buying process.

Other fashion shows produced by the apparel centers might include specialty shows for back-to-school, menswear or individual categories of merchandise. These fashion shows generally follow a pre-planned format. Music, clothing and accessories are changed to meet the current trends.

The Great Hall of the Dallas Apparel Mart provides a versatile forum for fashion presentations. The facility features a full-size stage, complete light and sound systems, seating for 4,000 auditorium style and 2,400 banquet style. An additional 1,500 to 3,000 people can view the stage from balconies overlooking the auditorium.

The apparel mart producers attempt to create a festive environment for the retail buyers. At the June Dallas Apparel Market featuring holiday merchandise, buyers were treated to a Christmas atmosphere complete with decorations, choirs singing Christmas carols and Santa Claus. Whatever the season, special events and gala fashion shows entertain the prospective buyers.

The Atlanta Apparel Mart has a minimum of three major production fashion shows during a four-day market. These ambitious shows feature 250 to 475 garments in a one hour production.

The California Mart with 2,000 showrooms is located in Los Angeles. Fashion shows for 500 people are held in the Fashion Theater. The Galleria, a lobby area, has space for an audience of 2,000.

The Chicago Market Center has two separate buildings. The Merchandise Mart features furniture and home furnishings. The newer Apparel Center is the space for apparel and accessory merchandise.

The Trade Association Show

Trade associations are groups of individuals and businesses acting as a professional, non-profit collective in meeting their common interests. Membership in trade associations provides a means for information exchange and political action to benefit the public opinion and legislative concerns. Trade associations represent almost every division of the fashion industry. These associations may be very specialized such as the *Jewelry Industry Council*, *Cotton Incorporated*, or the *Cosmetic, Toiletry and Fragrance Association*. Other associations focus on a broad or more generalized representation. The *American Apparel Manufacturers Association* and the *National Retail Federation* are examples of groups representing these general, total industry issues.

Among the various activities designed to enhance the image for the trade association members, fashion shows have long been used. The *Wool Bureau* regularly presents fashion shows to industry personnel. One extravaganza was the "Wool as Inspiration," a multi-media event held at a nightclub in New York City. The Wool Bureau set up live and video presentations to provide education and entertainment about wool. The *Polyester Fashion Council*, a consortium of six manufacturers of polyester, presented a fashion show at a National Retail Federation meeting emphasizing, "Polyester: It's a Fashion Natural." This was an attempt to alter the previously held attitude toward the product.

The Press Show

Press shows are held specifically for the members of the media prior to presenting the fashion story to the public—consumers. Members of the media represent magazines, newspapers, radio, television as well as wire services. Buyers, specially invited guests or important customers also may be invited to press shows. Only the largest designers, manufacturers, and retail firms present press shows. Stores may give a press show when a new department is opened, a designer visits the store, or a major promotion is launched. Manufacturers may invite the press to view a new line or product.

A press show must present new and exciting merchandise, since the press is in the business of reporting newsworthy events and products. The press show must be timed before the customers have seen the merchandise. One important reason for the press show is to create interest about the product or event beforehand.

Members of the press are routinely provided information about the merchandise, designer or event in the form of press kits, press releases and photographs. Some reporters will bring their own photographers for exclusive pictures.

The Men's Fashion Association trade show spotlighted an array of brand name microfibers. "Fashion & Microfibers— The Next Generation" was produced by the Polyester Council of America. (*WWD*)

RETAIL AND CONSUMER SHOWS

The Fashion Trend Show

At the retail level of distribution there is a fashion director who is responsible for providing fashion leadership and direction for that particular company. The fashion director prepares a detailed fashion forecast for the two major seasons: fall/winter and spring/summer. After visiting the major fashion centers, viewing the runway shows, and observing the trends from primary and secondary sources, the fashion director prepares a trend report. This trend report reflects the silhouettes, fabrics, colors, and themes for merchandise to be featured by the store represented. Since there are so many different possible combinations of merchandise available, the fashion director will provide a direction for the merchandising and promotion staff to follow. For example, when the color green is introduced in ready-to-wear, the fashion office should coordinate purchasing accessories and shoes of the same shade. Without some correlation, the ready-to-wear may feature olive green while the accessories and shoes may be hunter green.

With the major fashion trends identified, the fashion office will present a fashion trend show featuring the merchandise that illustrates the trend. This type of show is generally presented at the beginning of the season. Each segment of the show will feature one of the major trends.

Horne's Department Store and the Pittsburgh Symphony Association have combined efforts to produce a Fashion Gala for over 25 years. (Courtesy of Jane Vandenmade)

The In-store Fashion Show

As part of the ongoing education of sales personnel in a retail store, the in-store training fashion show is produced. These shows are most often presented in the morning before the store is opened.

After the fashion office has identified the major trends for a given season and the promotion office has planned various events and visual merchandising concepts, the store personnel are informed about the trends and timing of assorted promotions through an in-store training fashion show. These shows may be live or videotaped using managers and/or sales personnel as the models of the various trends. One important aspect of the in-store training show is to feature the merchandise trends from budget to designer price points. This enables the employees to adapt the look from all areas of the store. In-store training shows are never intended for the general public.

The timing of the seasonal trend show may coincide with the in-store training show. If this is the case, the trend show rehearsal may serve as the in-store training show.

The Consumer Show

The consumer fashion show is presented to the ultimate consumer, the person who buys garments and accessories for his or her personal use. Generally this type of show is presented by a retail store to a specific group of targeted customers.

Specialty Market Show One way the retail store is able to direct the product to a specific group of consumers is through specialty market fashion shows. Such a narrowly defined group may have a particular body type or special interests. Examples of specialty market shows might include: *Back-to-School, Bridal, Career, Children's, Cosmetics/Beauty, Hair, Lingerie, Menswear, Petite, Plus Sizes,* and *Swimwear.*

Back-to-School Fashion Show During the month of August some retail stores feature their back-to-school fashions during a consumer show. These shows are typically held in the store, often right in the children's apparel department. One such show that was held by the Higbee Company in Cleveland, Ohio, proclaimed, "School's Cool." This theme was carried through the department with signs and banners. The slogan was used in newspaper advertising and in credit card statements. These popular events frequently highlight the sons and daughters or grandchildren of store employees as models.

Bridal Fashion Show One type of specialty show that generates a lot of consumer interest is the Bridal Show, generally held twice each year. Shows for spring weddings are presented in December, January or February. Fall wedding shows are introduced during August or September. The retail bridal show frequently features a fashion show of bridal gowns, bridesmaids' gowns, and fashions for the entire wedding party. The bridal show also includes displays of products such as crystal, china, flatware, and small appliances necessary for setting up a new living arrangement. The event may also include representatives of services that will help to make the event a smooth one. Such services would include caterers, photographers, florists, beauty consultants, musicians, travel agencies, and so forth. Coordination of such an event is a large undertaking since presentations of these services must be related to the show itself.

Career Fashion Show Specialty shows that are produced for career women have increased in popularity during the last ten years. These shows have proven to be such audience grabbers that seats are often unattainable.

Cosmetics / Beauty and Hair Fashion Show Cosmetics, beauty, and hair are each important features of every fashion show. Some beauty salons and makeup studios encourage clothing retailers to take part in fashion shows created to emphasize makeup and hair trends.

Junior Fashion Show The junior market offers many appealing theme ideas for fashion shows. Since this specialty market has a strong interest in fashion and appearance, it is a well-accepted and well-attended type of show. Some of the different themes might include a slumber party, a pizza party, a collegiate party, or a holiday event.

Intimate Apparel Fashion Show Lingerie may be included in a general trend fashion show or it may be produced as a specialty market show. Christmas, Mother's Day, or Valentine's Day are preferred times of year to produce this type of specialty market fashion show.

Menswear Fashion Show Some retailers have responded to a growing interest in menswear with men's fashion shows. This market is generally produced during the peak seasons such as fall or spring.

Special Sizes Fashion Show With the rapidly expanding markets for special sizes, retailers and manufacturers have produced fashion shows for the petite and plus sizes. When the Liz Claiborne Corporation added a new product line for the plus size market, "Elisabeth," it was introduced to consumers through specialized fashion shows.

Holiday or Seasonal Fashion Show Seasonal fashion shows are designed to help consumers make the transition from one season to the next. After the Christmas holiday, one specialty market helps to relieve the winter doldrums.

Swimwear Fashion Show The swimwear market features the latest bathing suits. These shows help the audience to fantasize about the upcoming season.

BACK-TO-SCHOOL
BRIDAL
CAREER
CHILDREN'S APPAREL
COSMETICS / BEAUTY
HAIR
JUNIORS
LINGERIE
MEN'S WEAR
PETITES
PLUS SIZES
SWIMWEAR

Typical Specialty Market Shows

New Store Opening   A retailer will use a fashion show to introduce a new location including the store, personnel, and merchandise to the public. A fashion show for this event can generate excitement about the products and people associated with the new outlet.

Wardrobe Consulting   Personal image and wardrobe consulting are services provided by many retail organizations. A one-on-one consultation identifying personal attributes and flattering apparel and accessories is furnished. Almost any segment of a specialty market can use a wardrobe consulting fashion show to present fashions and fashion trends. General trends and fashion analysis provided for a particular body type was the theme of a recent fashion show. Petite models were dressed in regular clothing items from the store and "before" pictures were taken. At the show the models were dressed in clothing created for the petite market. The audience could see the "before" pictures on a large screen while the model wore clothing that fit her figure type. The before and after aspects of the makeover help to educate the consumer in improving her own personal appearance.

Home Sewing / Pattern Company / Fabric Store Fashion Show   Retail fabric stores feature fashions made from their fabrics in consumer fashion shows. The influential pattern manufacturers such as Vogue/Butterick, Simplicity, and McCall's work with fabric stores to present fashion shows featuring garments made from their patterns. Producers of notions such as zippers, thread, buttons, and trimmings work cooperatively with other companies involved in the home sewing industry.

Cooperative Fashion Show   The cooperative fashion show is presented as a joint effort between the retailer and primary or secondary manufacturer for the retail consumer. The cost of producing this type of show is shared by the manufacturer and the retailer. An example of this type of show would be a fashion show that features garments manufactured from a specific type of fiber. Another type of vendor co-sponsored show features a manufacturing company's representative as the guest commentator.

Benefit or Charity Fashion Show   Civic and philanthropic groups often sponsor fashion shows to generate funds for their activities. Money raised through ticket sales and donations are given to the charity identified by the show organizers. Sometimes local or national celebrity will serve as the commentator.

Cultural / Ethnic / Regional Fashion Show   A particular geographic location may have an opportunity to present a fashion show that features cultural, ethnic or simply regional fashions. An example of this type of show was the "Native American Fashion Show" presented at Northern Arizona University, Flagstaff, Arizona. This show was presented as a part of the Native American Cultural Heritage Week. The fashion show featured Native American models wearing contemporary fashions based upon regional ethnic designs.

MAGAZINE TIE-INS

Major fashion publications such as *W*, *Vogue*, *Glamour* and *Mademoiselle*, co-sponsor events held at retail locations. Magazine tie-in events are cooperatively produced by the retailer and the magazine to improve fashion awareness, to build traffic at the retail level and to increase the consumer's knowledge of the particular fashion publication. With

Retailers and fashion publications frequently co-produce special events such as this one cooperatively produced by W and Lord & Taylor, New York. Frequently magazines will also send editors to commentate (see page 118). *(W)*

increased shoppers visiting the store and heightened awareness of beauty and fashion trends, the fashion and cosmetics departments see immediate benefits.

Mademoiselle magazine's "On Location," feature is an example of a tie-in promotion. The merchandising editors of the magazine travel to important national retailers and coordinate the event with the store's fashion office. This event includes makeovers of audience volunteers, the latest fashion and beauty advice and a formal runway fashion show with professional models. The show features clothing from the store that fits the trends being featured in the magazine. The *Mademoiselle* editor and/or the store's fashion director can serve as commentator.

Another example of this type of show was the "*Glamour* in Sync" fashion shows cooperatively presented by *Glamour* magazine and Broadway Southwest Department Store. These events combined the themes and beauty trends as identified by *Glamour* with the clothing and trend fashion show produced by the Broadway Southwest fashion office. All of the stage set up, selection of clothing and models, and local coordination for the event was handled by the Broadway Southwest personnel. The show was commentated by Nancy Yberg, West Coast Merchandising Editor from *Glamour*, who flew into Phoenix with the Merchandising Editor from New York to represent the magazine.

In setting up such an event the magazine's merchandising or promotion department will send the store advance materials on "How To" produce the show and coordinate the related activities. This material will include detailed information on in-store announcements, publicity kits, promotional ideas, and advertising plans. A comprehensive outline on stage set-up, fashion show production and coordinated sales floor and window visual displays are also provided.

The Ebony **Fashion Fair** *Ebony* magazine sponsors a traveling fashion show. This show, known as the *Fashion Fair*, travels to approximately 190 different cities each year in the United States, Canada, and the Caribbean. The models, commentator, and crew move from one city to the next on a daily routine. The magazine's fashion staff visits many different

The *Ebony* Fashion Fair is the world's largest traveling fashion show raising money for black causes. Here models Rod Fuller and Deborah Laura model fashions from American and European designers. (NYT Pictures)

European and American designers, selecting merchandise to be featured in this traveling show. The show changes twice each year with the seasonal changes. This grueling schedule for the fashion show participants is a cooperative venture between the magazine fashion staff and hundreds of local charities. It serves as a fund-raising activity for the local group. Local charities invite the magazine to a particular city and takes care of all the regional needs, while the traveling crew sets up and takes down the show on a nightly basis.

Fashion shows are staged by a variety of organizations such as manufacturers, retailers, fashion schools and charitable groups. Shows range from simple informal modeling in a restaurant, showroom or store sales floor to an elaborate theatrical production requiring months of planning and preparation.

KEY FASHION SHOW TERMS

apparel mart	industrial show	press show
consumer fashion show	informal fashion show	production show
cooperative fashion show	in-store training fashion show	spectacular show
dramatized show	instructional video	tea-room modeling
fashion parade	magazine tie-in	trade association
fashion trend show	mannequin modeling	trade show
formal runway show	manufacturer's fashion show	trunk show
hatbox show	point-of-purchase video	video production

ADDITIONAL READINGS

1. Corinth, *Fashion Showmanship* (1970): The Types of Fashion Shows and What They Accomplish (Chapter 3) and The Specialized Fashion Show (Chapter 13).

2. Diehl, *How to Produce a Fashion Show* (1976): Types of Fashion Shows (Chapter 3) and Shows Requiring Special Handling (Chapter 13).

3. Guerin, *Creative Fashion Presentations* (1987): Fashion Shows in the Fiber and Fabric Industry (Chapter 2), Fashion Shows and the Garment Industry (Chapter 5), Fashion Shows and the Apparel Marts (Chapter 7), and Creative Presentations and Fashion Shows at the Retail Level (Chapter 10).

Advance Planning

A dvance planning involves all aspects of preliminary preparation necessary to present a well-executed show. Planning must be appropriate to the purpose of the show and the abilities of the group producing the show. Fall school clothes should be the focus of a back-to-school fashion show, using children as models and attracting parents and children as the audience. Charity shows should be planned keeping in mind the purpose to raise money but not overpricing the tickets to the show for the intended audience. A group attempting their first fashion show may opt to hold an informal or trunk show rather than a production show using live music and dancers. It is better to do an excellent job on a small show than a mediocre job on a large show.

Advance planning is the organization of the show, including working out the many details such as selecting the appropriate leadership. The leaders in turn delegate responsibilities, foresee problems which may occur, and continually review the progress of the show. The size of the show may determine the location. The lifestyle of the audience may dictate the theme. A service organization may have a planned audience but no theme or location. A retail store may have a planned storewide theme but may need to concentrate on a target market.

Without advance planning unexpected problems occur which could easily be avoided. Communication is very important to advance planning. Lines of communication among the fashion show producers must be well defined and functional or advance planning will be of no benefit to planning the show.

AUDIENCE

Planning a fashion show must include determining who the audience will be. Many times the audience will determine the purpose of the event. The audience may consist of fashion-

Figure 3-1
An organization chart
(facing page) to illustrate
fashion show leadership
and responsibilities. Key:
Boxes are used to designate
the people involved with a
fashion show activity;
circles represent an action
executed with written
evidence.

able, conservative, or career oriented individuals. The merchandise selected for the show must match the audience in order to promote appropriate trends to the audience.

The audience may take two different forms, **guaranteed** or **created audience**. An audience that is established before the show is organized is considered a guaranteed audience, individuals who will attend the show regardless of the fashions displayed. A show that is presented at an annual meeting of an organization with an existing membership list is considered a guaranteed audience.

An audience which is established after the show is planned as a result of publicity and advertising is considered a created audience. A retailer may use a fashion show to attract an audience for the premiere of a new department. The retailer is creating a new audience by producing a show that meets the needs of the audience. This audience is very concerned with the type of fashions displayed.

An audience may be gathered from many different sources. Department stores may use mailing lists of customers. Communities with local business or social organizations may share their membership lists. Local fashion students from universities, colleges and high schools are always an eager audience. Advertising will be aimed at the general public, however, fashion shows are generally more successful when a specific audience is attracted rather than the general public off the street. Age, gender, income, and career of the targeted audience must be appraised. Other considerations are the interests and lifestyle of the audience, and the occasion and/or season for which the show is being held.

Audience Size

The size of the audience often determines the type of show, although, the type of show can in some instances determine the size of the audience. All members of the audience need to be able to easily view the fashions from a comfortable location. A production or runway show may be required if the audience is large, filling a grand ballroom or an auditorium. Small audiences allow a more intimate environment between the models and the audience, therefore an informal show setting within a retail store or restaurant as the location may be appropriate. If it is necessary to limit the number of people attending a fashion show, reserved tickets or RSVP's may be required.

Audience Age

Consider the age of the audience when planning a show. Young audiences need to be entertained with plenty of action; in theater productions this may be referred to as "business." It is also necessary to have louder, more contemporary music with a faster beat for a younger crowd. A more mature crowd is usually more interested in the merchandise than younger audiences and wants very explicit, detailed commentary. The music must be softer and non-offensive. If the audience is mixed, the show should appeal to many age groups, not offensively loud to turn off people, or slow to the point of boredom for the younger population.

Audience Income

If selling merchandise is the primary reason for producing a show then it is important to be aware of the income of the audience. Retailers know the approximate spending habits of

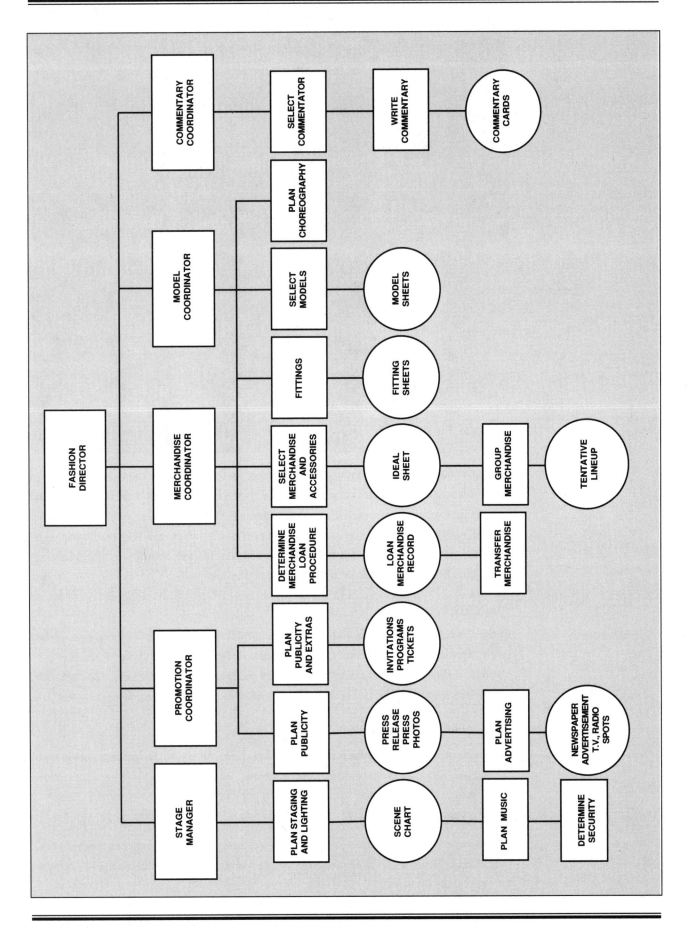

A *Glamour* editor commentates this show. The advance planning for the event is accomplished by the local retailer and the store's fashion director.

their customers, and this should be reviewed before selecting the merchandise. Merchandise that is too expensive or has the appearance of being too expensive will intimidate customers because they will feel embarrassed that they cannot afford to purchase anything. On the other hand, merchandise that is inexpensive in the eyes of the audience will be overlooked as a nonstatus item. Fashions ill-matched to the audience will lose both immediate sales and future sales because the audience will not return to the store.

Audience Gender

Consider whether the audience will purchase the displayed merchandise for themselves or for others. Specialty stores, featuring gift merchandise, offer men's night before Christmas and Valentine's Day. These fashion shows can be very successful promotional tools. The store may offer a discount within a limited period of time, greatly improving audience response.

Audience Occupations

Review the careers of the audience members. Are the members of the audience looking for transitional clothing to wear to the office or are they looking for strictly recreational clothing? Some customers may feel they can spend more money if the garments will be used for business versus pleasure.

It is important to review all of the points discussed above regarding the audience when planning a show. Forgetting one element can change the atmosphere of the show and decrease the opportunity for sales.

LEADERSHIP

Good organization and management of fashion shows is dependent on good leadership. Two forms of leadership include fashion directors and fashion show coordinators. A retail store may have a fashion director, an individual responsible for creating the fashion image for that particular retailer. The fashion director is responsible for selecting silhouettes, colors, and fabrics for the upcoming seasons and establishing a sense of fashion leadership for the store to the public. Fashion show production plays a major role in the job of a fashion director. A school production or civic organization may have a fashion show coordinator or co-coordinators. A fashion show coordinator is the individual charged with the responsibility of producing the show, planning all arrangements, delegating responsibilities, and accepting accountability for all details. In school productions and civic organizations the

```
            October 25-Things To Do

Gather supplies for dressing Rooms - Pam
        Pins
        Needles
        Tape
        Paper, Pens

Finish Commentary — Trina, Debbie, Kathleen

Check Sunday Paper for Ad — me

Monday
Technical Run Through
   Check lights — Mike
   Music — Dave
   Stage — Stephanie, Julie

Set should be complete — Stephanie, Julie

Check late RSVP'S!!

flowers
   table decorations

reserve seating for new fashion editor
```

Figure 3-2
Page from Fashion
Director's Diary

coordinator may be elected or appointed by the group members. In some cases experts may be called in to organize the show such as with the shows produced by *Ebony* Magazine.

A fashion show coordinator must have several traits. The coordinator must be able to communicate with all parties involved both verbally and in writing. Verbal information may not be enough communication. Written communication must be stressed. Information should be put in writing so that individuals are aware of details. People often give directions verbally in a hurried manner only to forget the directions later; written communication allows both parties to refer back to what directions were assigned. Additionally, the coordinator must keep a written **diary** or record of all plans for the show. This diary serves as a reminder to the coordinator of tasks to be completed, follow-up dates, and future needs of the show. The diary may also be a helpful tool if an organization decides to produce another show in the future.

The show coordinator must communicate planning activities to all concerned individuals. Of course the audience should be informed but other individuals who have a vested interest in the show should not be ignored. A retailer should inform all salespeople far in advance of the details of the show so that they may promote the event to their customers. A school group or civic organization must pass information to all members so that they may tell others wishing to attend.

A fashion show coordinator must be able to foresee show problems and be flexible to work around these problems and/or inconveniences. Many problems occur during critical moments of the show and must be dealt with in a professional and timely manner. Common problems include models or merchandise exchanges right before the show causing changes in commentary and lineup.

The fashion show coordinator must continually review the progress of the show, making sure the show is running smoothly and deadlines are met. Many people are involved in the show and it is important for the show coordinator to know everything that the others are doing.

Delegating Responsibilities

When planning a fashion show, the show coordinator must delegate certain responsibilities to others. Each show coordinator will divide responsibilities differently depending on the complexity of the show. Production shows may require many area coordinators with specialized responsibilities while a trunk show may only require one or two area coordinators with varied responsibilities.

Model Coordinator One area of responsibility that a show coordinator often delegates is the organization of models. A **model coordinator** is responsible for selecting and training the models, and coordinating activities that involve the models. Additional areas of responsibilities for the model coordinator may include supervising a female and a male model coordinator, a model workshop coordinator for inexperienced models, and makeup, hair, or other beauty technicians.

Staging Coordinator Most shows require the services of a **stage manager**. The stage manager oversees use of the stage and runway, organizes equipment, and supervises people providing services behind the scenes, such as a properties manager, stage hands, music, microphone and lighting technicians. Some facilities such as city auditoriums have a stage manager on their staffs and require that they be hired by the group when the location is rented.

Promotion Coordinator Most fashion shows require promotion. Show coordinators may delegate these responsibilities to the advertising department if one is available or select a **promotion coordinator** and a **program editor**. The promotion coordinator is accountable for the creation and distribution of promotional materials for the show including press releases, press photographs, tickets, invitations, commercials, signage, table decorations, and other forms of promotion. The promotion coordinator may also supervise a coordinator or hostess to fulfill these obligations. The promotion coordinator may additionally perform public relations activities. This coordinator may hire a photographer for services before and during the show.

A **program editor** is responsible for all activities related to creating a program. This includes the design, and printing of the program, distribution of the program and the solicitation of advertisements to pay for the program.

Other Coordinators Depending on the intricacy of the show other people may be needed to participate in the fashion show production. These additional areas of responsibilities would include merchandise coordinator and commentary coordinator.

When delegating responsibilities, all available resources, personnel, and services should be considered. A show coordinator must have a sense about people to determine how well they

MODEL COMMITTEE

FEMALE MODEL COORDINATOR

MALE MODEL COORDINATOR

MODEL WORKSHOP COORDINATOR

HAIR TECHNICIAN

BEAUTY TECHNICIAN

CHOREOGRAPHER

STAGING COMMITTEE

MUSIC DIRECTOR

MUSIC TECHNICIAN

PROPS MANAGER

BACKSTAGE MANAGER

SOUND TECHNICIAN

SECURITY

LIGHTING TECHNICIAN

STAGE MANAGER

MUSICIANS

ELECTRICIANS

PROMOTION COMMITTEE

PROGRAM EDITOR

ADVERTISING COORDINATOR

PUBLICITY COORDINATOR

PUBLIC RELATIONS COORDINATOR

PHOTOGRAPHER

TICKET CHAIR

INVITATION CHAIR

TABLE DECORATIONS/SEATING HOSTESS

MERCHANDISE COMMITTEE

FITTINGS MANAGER

LINEUP MANAGER

STARTERS

DRESSERS CUE PERSONNEL

DRESSING ROOM SUPERVISOR (SECURITY)

COMMENTARY COMMITTEE

COMMENTATOR

COMMENTARY WRITER

ANNOUNCER

List of the various committees including the chair and members.

Figure 3-3

Responsibility Sheet

RESPONSIBILITY SHEET

Show Theme _____

Location _____

Day _____

Date _____

Time _____

Confirmed by _____   Phone _____

Contact Person at Location _____   Phone _____

Type of Merchandise _____

Merchandise Chair _____   Phone _____

Specific Categories   Category Titles

1. _____

2. _____

3. _____

4. _____

5. _____

6. _____

Models

Model Chair _____   Phone _____

Number of models _____

Model Resources _____

Contact Person at Agency _____   Phone _____

Promotion

Promotion Chair _____   Phone _____

Type of Promotions Used   Completion Dates

1. _____

2. _____

3. _____

Designer _____   Phone _____

Printer _____   Phone _____

Staging

Stage Manager_____   Phone _____

Type of Production _____

Supplies Needed _____   Completion Date _____

Props Needed _____   Completion Date _____

Music Selection _____   Completion Date _____

Commentator _____   Phone _____

will followthrough with assigned work. Sometimes the best available people are volunteers rather than individuals paid to perform a task. However, there are volunteers who will not take their responsibilities seriously. Enthusiasm must be proven in actions not words.

Responsibility Sheet

A responsibility sheet is a helpful tool in planning a show and delegating responsibilities to all participants. The show coordinator records each delegated task on the responsibility sheet, then distributes copies of this form to coordinators so that all individuals may know who is accountable for each task.

THEME

Fashion shows should have a theme and title, which will tell the audience the nature of the fashion show, and should be selected during the planning stages. The theme can be developed around the targeted audience or around the merchandise selected. It allows the publicity, the merchandise, and other planning elements to be joined to show continuity.

Where do theme ideas come from? Probably the easiest theme idea will develop from a season or a holiday. Lingerie shows are always popular around Valentine's Day, just as back-to-school promotional shows are the hit in August and September. Special occasion or holiday and resort wear are common in November and December. If a holiday has been overused then look to current events to create a theme. Current music or art trends may lend themselves to a theme particularly if the music or art is popular with the selected audience. Spring always brings about travel ideas with themes centering around geographic locations. "Get Away" shows exhibiting tropical paradises always attract large audiences. Specific color themes or a special interest of the audience may also be an easy theme to develop. The outdoor atmosphere may be perfect for a sporting goods fashion show attracting a certain audience to the event. "Compositions in Style," "So Many Clothes, So Little Time," or "The Professional You!" are examples of fashion shows with imaginative or creative themes.

Fashion show themes relating to the type of show being presented might include Bridal Gala, Symphony Fashion Jubilee, or the Junior League Soiree. Themes could also be related to the designer presenting the fashions. The *Geoffrey Beene Collections* or *Breakfast with Donna Karan* reflect designer themes. When a fashion show is sponsored by a vendor, publication, or organization, it is often a courtesy to include the sponsor in the theme. It not only promotes the vendor but can also pull in a larger audience if the vendor is well known.

Fashion shows are divided into segments depending on the merchandise selected. After a theme has been developed each segment or scene can be created to coordinate with the chosen title.

LOCATION

Will the audience travel a long or short distance to view the show? Production shows or runway shows are often used when the audience has to travel a longer distance. The audi-

Figure 3-4
Time Line of
Responsibilities

Responsibility	Time Allotment Before Show	
	Earliest Planning	**Latest Planning**
Select Show Director	6 months	5 weeks
Decide Show Theme, Location, Audience	5 months	5 weeks
Plan Budget	5 months	5 weeks
Select Show Co-Chair	5 months	5 weeks
Reserve Location	5 months	5 weeks
Plan Seating Arrangement	1 month	week of show
Technical Run-through	1 week	1 day
Dress Rehearsal	1 week	day of show
Strike Show	day of show	
Evaluation	1 day after show	1 week after show
Model Committee		
Select Models	3 months	3 weeks
Prepare Tentative Lineup	1 month	2 weeks
Set Choreography	1 month	week of show
Merchandise Committee		
Plan Merchandise Groupings/Scenes	4 months	3 weeks
Review Merchandise	3 months	2 weeks
Prepare Tentative Lineup	1 month	2 weeks
Fittings	2 weeks	week of show
Pull Merchandise	week of show	
Prepare Final Lineup	week of show	
Transfer Merchandise	1 week	day of show
Return Merchandise	day of show	1 day after show
Commentary Committee		
Prepare Filler Commentary	5 months	2 weeks
Write Commentary	1 month	week of show
Staging Committee		
Begin Music Selection	4 months	3 weeks
Prepare Set	3 months	2 weeks
Publicity Committee		
To Printer: Program Cover, Flyer, Invitation, Tickets	3 months	3 weeks
Plan Advertising	3 months	2 weeks
Write Press Release	2 months	3 weeks
Send Press Release	6 weeks	2 weeks
Distribute Flyers	6 weeks	2 weeks
Run In-store Advertising	6 weeks	week of show
Send Invitations	1 month	2 weeks
To Printer: Program Contents	1 month	10 days
Run Newspaper Advertising	1 month	week of show
Write Thank You Notes	1 day after show	1 week after show

ence may feel they are getting "more for their money" for the distance traveled if they view a production or runway show rather than an informal show. There are areas of the United States where more than one climate dominates. It is important to decide which climate will be represented or how to combine merchandise suited for both climates in a compatible way. Are you going to hold the show in a hotel, restaurant, auditorium? On the retail floor? In the manufacturer's showroom?

Working with a Hotel

The member of the fashion show committee responsible for working with the hotel should make an appointment to speak with the hotel representative as soon as possible. The individual in charge of hotel sales may have such titles as Sales or Marketing Manager, Coordinator or Director. Depending upon the size and type of hotel there may be one or more people directly involved in the services relating to Banquets and Catering or Sales and Marketing.

It is best to have some simple qualifying questions ready prior to the first meeting. Some qualifying questions to have ready when making the appointment include:

1. Is there a specific date when the show is to be held or is the date somewhat flexible?
2. What is the size of the audience?
3. What type of seating arrangements will be needed?
4. Will food service take place in the same location as the fashion show?
5. What sound and lighting systems, staging, and dressing area facilities are available?

Fashion show producers should not hesitate to work with hotel professionals. The sales directors will assist them in every aspect of planning as it relates to room rental and food and beverage service. Other services may include setting up, serving, and cleaning up. All of the details do not have to be worked out in advance.

There are additional concerns in relationship to the physical facilities. The number of people that are able to attend may be limited by the size of the room. However, work with the type of hotel that can offer the services desired by the group. If a room for an audience of 250 is needed, but the hotel can only handle 100 people it does not make any sense to waste the time of the hotel personnel. The hotel should be able to provide tables, tablecloths, serving dishes, plates, glasses, flatware, and napkins. Some hotels, particularly in larger cities may be able to provide various seating arrangements from theater style to luncheon style. Extra amenities might include runways, stages, public address systems, projectors, VCR's, stereo systems and technicians.

Hotels rarely permit people to use caterers or to "self-cater" events. Outside food service preparation has generally been a hassle for hotel personnel and health regulations or state laws prohibit this type of activity.

Alcoholic beverages may also be served to a fashion show audience. If the hotel has a liquor license, it may be against state laws to serve alcohol other than through the hotel's service. The hotel could set up a cash or hosted bar. If alcohol is to be served, some states require that the tickets state who is eligible to drink the beverages. Depending upon the state laws a special permit may be obtained for serving wine for a fund-raising activity. An

Arizona hotel handled this scenario by requiring that the wine be donated for the nonprofit cause. A special one-day use permit was granted by the Arizona State Liquor Board allowing the hotel to serve the wine donated by the local distributor for a charity event.

At the time the arrangements are finalized a contract should be written. Fashion show planners should be suspicious if a contract is not required. It protects both the hotel and the organization using their services.

Working with a Restaurant

Many of the concerns relevant to working with a restaurant are similar to those discussed when working with a hotel. One of the main differences is in regard to a contract—a restaurant may not require a contract.

Restaurants or cocktail lounges may allow fashion show producers to use their facilities as long as the show does not interrupt normal business activities. Owners and managers of such establishments recognize that a fashion show may increase traffic to their site.

A common use for a restaurant is for informal modeling provided by a local retailer during the lunch hour. This would not require the use of a commentator, specialized music, or a large technical staff.

Problems to consider before using a restaurant or lounge for a fashion show might include health regulations and the age of the participants. Dressing rooms cannot be placed in or near kitchen areas as required by state health officials. Fashion show staff under legal drinking age may not be allowed at the facility during certain business hours.

Serving Food and Beverages

Food served to the audience depends upon a number of conditions including the type of show being presented. Service may be as simple as providing beverages or as elaborate as a multiple course meal.

Retail organizations trying to attract the customer interested in business apparel have tried breakfast and box lunch shows. These shows feature a simple and attractive breakfast or lunch during the time this customer traditionally shops or prior to going to the office. Tying meal time to the entertainment of the fashion show, often educating the customer as well, has proven to be a popular approach to attracting this type of client.

Charitable organizations like to include a social element to the formal fashion presentation. A cocktail hour and/or meal before or after the presentation are a preferred method of combining the two activities.

Most restaurants, hotels or other facilities require using their food and beverage services. When selecting the location for the fashion show this limitation should be discussed. If there are no such restraints from the location management, it may be appropriate to work with any caterer.

Working with a Caterer

A retail store or a manufacturer presenting a fashion show at their own location is more likely to work directly with a caterer for food service. A runway may be set up on the retail sales floor where the merchandise is located. A manufacturer may show the collection right

S	M	T	W	TH	F	S
29	**30** Decide on Show theme, audience, location Director, Budget	**31**	**1** Select co-chairmen / Reserve location & food service	**2** merchandise overview	**3**	**4**
5	**6** Plan merchandise groupings/scenes	**7** Write Press Release / Take Press Photographs	**8** Select models / Begin music selections	**9** Program cover, flyers, invitations tickets to printer	**10**	**11**
12	**13** Send invitations / Send press release / Distribute flyers / Confirm advertising	**14** review merchandise for last minute additions	**15** Arrange security / Plan Decorations	**16**	**17** Tentative line-up / Have filler commentary prepared	**18** Program inside to printer
19 Run Newspaper advertising	**20** Model workshops to set choreography / run in store / Build set ——>	**21**	**22** reconfirm location / advertising / RSVP due	**23** Pull merchandise / Plan seating / Have props gathered	**24** Fittings Stage complete / Confirm food service & location / Write commentary	**25** Confirm final line-up / gather dressing room materials
26 Run Newspaper advertising	**27** Build set on location / technical run through / Confirm security	**28** Transfer merchandise / DRESS REHERSAL / finalize seating & decorations	**29** SHOW / strike show	**30** Return merchandise & accessories / evaluation / Write thank you's	**1**	**2**

Figure 3-5
Fashion Show Planning Calendar

in the showroom. In these cases the services of a hotel or restaurant are not needed. A caterer should be able to provide the fashion show planners with samples of their work and information about the type of clients and food served in the past. Photographs of prior parties or events should be able to give the fashion show planners an idea of how previous events were handled. Generally caterers will provide the names of patrons who have used their services. It is a good idea to check some of these references or check with other people who have used a particular caterer.

A contract should be prepared to protect both the caterer and the fashion show producers. It should explain what will be served, the costs, and any other obligations of the caterer.

TIMING

In planning a fashion show timing certain activities of the show is crucial and often poorly planned. Poor planning will cause havoc as the show draws closer.

First, the day, date, and time of the show must be set. This must be established when the location is being determined so as to coordinate all efforts. A location which is only accessible during business hours should not be chosen if the show must be held in the evening.

Time of the show must be set so that all participants and audience members can allocate traveling time to and from the show. Check for possible conflicts with other events. Avoid selecting a day that is already filled with other community activities.

Some shows are developed six months in advance while others are prepared days in advance. A timetable should be created with deadlines so all individuals can work together.

Individuals within the fashion industry are familiar with the Fashion Calendar. This weekly calendar serves as a guide for retailers, manufacturers, and the press to keep industry insiders aware of market weeks. It provides a clearing house for dates and relevant information regarding key national and international fashion events, helping to avoid potential conflicts.

Length of the Fashion Show

The length of the fashion show also should be established. Usually this is determined by the number of outfits in the show. A show within a retail store should last no longer than 45 minutes, for the attention span of an audience only lasts about this long. The show should be paced with one or two outfits per minute allowing the audience time to thoroughly review each outfit. If the audience is more fashion forward they may be able to view more clothes in a shorter period of time, and absorb more fashion trends. A younger audience dictates a faster paced show.

SECURITY

The security of merchandise and equipment are primary factors when producing a fashion show but may be overlooked in the show preparation. The security of the audience and show personnel must also be investigated to insure safety of the participants and protect the show against legal damages. Protection of people and materials should be reviewed as the show is finalized. To protect all individuals involved in transactions of merchandise, equipment, locations, or any other materials, agreements should be put in writing and signed by both show personnel and the leasing agent for the location and the merchandise.

Merchandise Security

Merchandise on loan from retailers for the rehearsals and show is the responsibility of the show staff. It must be protected from damage while it is being worn and from theft or vandalism.

Consumer shows on location away from a retail store have special concerns regarding theft. The nature of fashion shows permits many individuals to have access to the stage and dressing areas where merchandise is located during the show preparation and performance. Consequently, merchandise while it is away from the merchant, should be protected from show personnel and others. Show personnel should always be aware of all necessary staff and question any unfamiliar bystanders. Hiring professional models and technicians may cause less concern than the use of amateurs.

One person or one committee should be assigned the responsibility for organizing, labeling, transferring and securing the merchandise from the retail store to the show location. This committee should also know what personnel may have direct contact with the merchandise.

Figure 3-5

Sample Security Contract

```
                    SECURITY CONTRACT


(date)
    On (fill in date of show) a fashion show will be
presented by (group) at (location). The show will
display merchandise from local merchants and benefit
the (fill in name of group/organization).
    Upon departure from the retail store, the merchan-
dise will be the responsibility of the Show Director.
She will be accountable for the merchandise until it
is returned to e retailer after the Show.
    I, the undersigned, realize that I am responsible
for caring for each garment carefully and profession-
ally. If a garment or accessory is missing or dam-
aged, it will be my responsibility to report the
items to the Merchandise Chairperson immediately. I
will be accountable for any unreported merchandise.



               _____ Signed
                           _____ Date
```

Shows using amateur personnel, models or dressers, may have these individuals sign waivers that they will be responsible for missing or damaged merchandise. This contract may not hold up in court, but it encourages and strengthens a sense of responsibility.

Design Piracy Beyond merchandise security against theft or damage, couture or prestige merchandise must be protected against *design piracy*. Stealing designs and creating "*knock-offs*," or copies of designer originals at lower prices, are so commonplace in the fashion industry that European designers hire security agents during collection openings. The agents do not allow any individuals to see the collection until it is presented on the runway. Timing is crucial in the presentation of these design ideas. They are so secret that a show could be ruined if the design ideas were leaked before the proper time.

Location and Equipment Security

Show staff also have the responsibility of securing the location and any borrowed or leased equipment. *Lease agreements*, contracts between leasing agency and users, should be drawn up before the show. If necessary, security personnel should be hired to keep watch of the equipment.

Insurance Hotels, auditoriums, restaurants, and other locations may provide insurance policies to cover the show. The show coordinator should know where the responsibility for fashion show insurance lies, with the show or with the location. If insurance is provided make sure it covers the period of time when the merchandise is transported from the showroom to the show location. The policy should also cover the audience and personnel of the show against accidents or injury as a result of the fashion show. If the location does not provide insurance the fashion show committee may wish to take out a policy to protect merchandise, equipment, personnel, and guests of the show. It is better to have coverage than leave the show organization open to lawsuits that may be very costly.

Audience Security

The audience must also feel safe at the location and be protected from equipment used during the show. Electrical cords used for sound equipment or lighting that crosses audience walkways should be taped securely to the floor. It is necessary for show personnel to make sure fire codes have been met at the location. Fire extinguishers and other safety equipment should be located. Entrances and exits should be marked for the audience in case of emergency. Aisles should be spaced properly to allow for easy access.

Security should never be overlooked in show preparation. Legally, the show director is responsible for accidents or injuries of the audience; professionally the director must assure the safety of the garments and accessories; personally, the director must show confidence to the staff and crew that safety will be assured.

It is a mistake to overlook advance planning and not put a lot of effort into the fashion show. The more planning that goes into the show the more confidence the show director and fashion show staff will have when it comes time to present the fashions. Advance planning will not prevent all problems associated with fashion show production, but it will help to eliminate many concerns.

KEY FASHION SHOW TERMS

advance planning	fashion show coordinator	program editor
created audience	guaranteed audience	promotion coordinator
design piracy	knock-off	responsibility sheet
Fashion Calendar	lease agreement	stage manager
fashion director	model coordinator	theme

ADDITIONAL READINGS

1. Corinth, *Fashion Showmanship* (1970): Planning a Compatible Show and Audience (Chapter 4), Selecting the Place for the Show (Chapter 5), and How to Plan and Organize the Show (Chapter 6).

2. Diehl, *How to Produce a Fashion Show* (1976): Background and Advance Planning (Chapter 4).

3. Goschie, *Fashion Direction and Coordination* (1986): Planning Fashion Shows (Chapter 6).

4. Guerin, *Creative Fashion Presentations* (1987): Work sheet: fashion show check list for market week trade show (pp 144-149) and tips for holding a store fashion show (pp 310-314).

4

Planning the Budget

Many inexperienced fashion show producers think that fashion shows cost little or nothing to produce. Even informal shows can involve some substantial costs. As the show becomes more elaborate and complex the costs increase. The **budget** is an estimate of the revenues and expenses necessary to produce the fashion show. It is the best guess of what will be included in the costs and income from ticket sales or vendor cooperative financial support. The budget must remain flexible, an essential part of the forecasting and planning process, since there may be some unexpected or hidden costs. Budget revisions need to take place if circumstances change.

The type of show being produced, audience, location, and special features of the show are directly dependent upon the amount of funds available in the budget. The least expensive type of show to produce is an informal show presented right at the point of sale, the manufacturer's showroom, or the retail sales floor. The most expensive shows are large benefit programs or specialized couture shows for private customers and the fashion trade. These shows require large numbers of support staff as well as hotel and equipment rentals. Some of the top designer fashion shows have been reported to cost over a half million and up to a million dollars. One example of an extravagant designer show was the spring 1984 Perry Ellis fashion spectacular *(Vogue, 1984)*. This show was presented in two one-hour productions to retail buyers and the fashion press. Thirty-six male and female photographic models, charging a minimum of $500 per hour, were hired to present the collection consisting of 168 outfits. Each model was chosen to fit a certain illusion. There were 36 dressers hired to help the models change. Makeup, hair, nails, and the models' walk were planned to compliment the proper image. Hair specialist Gerard Bollei and his staff created hairstyles. Makeup was administered by Bonnie Maller and an assistant. Music, sound, lighting, security, and catering were handled by separate crews. In addition there was a crew to set up

An elaborate production show has a number of expenses. This 1984 Perry Ellis fashion spectacular (top) was reported to cost over half a million dollars. Zoran (bottom) produced a show in 1984 with minimal expense. Models informally presented clothing in the designer's showroom. (*WWD*)

bleachers at the showroom. Invitations and RSVP's were controlled by three assistants employed just for that job. A calligrapher was engaged to make seating cards. As many as a dozen part-time sample makers were brought in to help finish the garments. A photographer, graphic designer, and printer were given the responsibility of producing the program and invitations. A caterer was engaged to feed the large staff. A video crew was hired to record the lavish event. Flower arrangements as well as fashion accessories were created by specialists, eminent in their field, just for this show. Over one hundred people were involved in presenting this show, estimated to cost over a half million dollars, one of the more expensive designer shows to be presented at this time. Every detail was overseen by Perry Ellis, the late designer.

At the opposite end of the expense scale, designer Zoran presented a more modest show, also in 1984. Five models informally modeled the clothes in the designer's Washington D.C. showroom without runways, props, or theatrics. The only extravagance was lunch—flown in by Zoran from New York's famous gourmet food shop Balducci.

Regardless of the extravagance of a show, fashion show planners must evaluate all of the various expenses involved in producing the show during the initial stages of planning. In order to achieve the goals set for the production, the budget process must be approached in a methodical manner.

THE BUDGETARY PROCESS

Manufacturers and retailers work well in advance of their selling season in preparing budget forecasts. For example retailers budget for two six-month periods—February to July and August to January. Budgets are prepared as much as 90 days prior to the start of the season. The marketing/merchandising team from a retail or manufacturing firm anticipates the sales volume or revenue for the company as the first step in the **budgeting process**. Based upon this estimate all other aspects of the financial planning take place. One such aspect is the appropriation of funds for all of its sales promotion activities. The amount can vary depending upon the type of company and type of product. Retailers commonly base this appropriation as one to four percent of anticipated annual sales. Apparel manufacturers typically appropriate a higher percentage of annual sales to promotional activities than do retailers spending as much as five to ten percent. The cosmetic and fragrance industries commit the highest percent to promotional activities, as much as 20 to 25 percent of annual sales. The fashion director has a good idea of the limitations and expectations set by budgets. Civic groups intending to plan fashion shows as one of the group's functions should follow the lead of the retail and manufacturing companies in setting up budgets in advance of the show planning.

The budgeting process may be accomplished using three different methods:
1. top-down approach
2. bottom-up approach
3. all-one-can-afford approach

Top-down Approach

In the top-down method the promotional budget allocations are determined by upper or senior management who have access to the organization's overall financial picture (or by the executive committee for a club). Their knowledge is based on their past experience and involvement in determining all key monetary decisions including goals and estimates.

Using the top-down approach assumes that there is some experience or past history that can be used as a guide. It also allows the upper management to exercise tight control of promotion expenses. Typically large, well-established firms with good historical records use this type of budgeting.

The top-down approach does have its limitations. It does not always reflect the knowledge and concerns of the day-to-day operational managers. Therefore without their participation in decision-making, there may not be a personal commitment by the people central to reaching goals.

Bottom-up Approach

The bottom-up method of budgeting requires the operational managers (or committee chairs of an organization) to establish the expenses related to their areas of responsibility. For example the chair of the model committee estimates the costs relating to hiring, fitting, and training models. The fashion director pulls together each committee's expense estimates to finalize the budget. An advantage of the bottom-up method is teamwork. People who have input into the process are likely to take ownership and accountability for their jobs. This approach helps to overcome the limitations discussed in the top-down approach by allowing division or department heads (or committee chairs) to participate in the planning process. It invites input from the people who will be responsible for the success of the project.

The bottom-up method is rarely used in large corporations since it is time-consuming and difficult to coordinate. Large companies generally do not like to give up centralized control of budgetary concerns.

All-One-Can-Afford Approach

The philosophy here is to spend what is necessary to meet the competition. Periodic evaluation of sales volume is used by the firm to determine what the firm can afford to spend. This is the least scientific and perhaps the least professional method of allocating promotional budgets. The all-one-can-afford method is rarely used by large fashion related businesses.

Each company or organization should determine the best method of allocating promotional budgets based upon its specific goals and objectives. A combination of the methods may best serve the group's needs.

THE PROMOTIONAL PLAN

After the promotion appropriation is determined, the budget is then allocated to the different promotional activities. A marketing/merchandising team for the manufacturer or retailer decides where to place the emphasis and how much of the promotion budget should go to

MONTH _October_   **YEAR** _199X_

SUNDAY	MONDAY	TUESDAY	WEDNESDAY	THURSDAY	FRIDAY	SATURDAY
	1	2 Tea-Room Modeling 11-1	3	4	5	6 Children's Dept. 2 PM Osh Kosh
7	8 COLUMBUS DAY COAT SALE/ SHOW Coat Dept. 6 PM	9 Tea-Room Modeling 11-1	10	11 LAUNCH OF ELIZABETH 6 PM	12	13
14 CAREER	15 WEEK LIZ CLAIBORNE NOON	16 Tea-Room Modeling 11-1	17 EVAN PICONE NOON	18 BRECKENRIDGE NOON	19 JONES NEW YORK NOON	20 CAREER WEEK Show/ Better Apparel 2 PM Dept.
21 MAJOR SALE: ANNIVERSARY SALE	22	23 Tea-Room Modeling 11-1	24	25 JUNIOR LEAGUE COUNTRY CLUB HOLIDAY FASHION PREMIERE 1:30 PM	26	27
28 ANNIVERSARY SALE	29	30 Tea-Room Modeling 11-1	31			

advertising, publicity, visual merchandising, special events or fashion shows. Each specific area of sales promotion develops its plan for action based upon the objectives and strategies of the promotion division.

Figure 4-1
Retail Fashion Show
Calendar

The Fashion Show Budget

Once the promotional budget is set the fashion director or designated executive plans the fashion show schedule. The **fashion show plan** is a schedule for a specific period of time, commonly six months or a year, for all of the fashion shows that a firm intends to produce. The fashion show plan includes the following information:

- a planning calendar
- divisions, departments, products or services targeted for fashion show participation
- estimated costs

The planning calendar consists of the dates, times, and places for fashion shows. As much detail as possible is used to outline the time frame necessary to plan and produce all fashion shows for a particular season.

The first step in planning the budget for a fashion show is to consider all of the possible expenditures. The fashion show director or the person delegated this responsibility should get estimates for the various costs. Written estimates should be provided for large expenses such as site fees and catering. Each show will incur a specific set of expenses. For example, there is generally no expense relating to site fee if the show is held in the retail store or manufacturer's showroom. This plan for expenditures should be updated as the actual expenses are incurred. These records should be kept for a final accounting of the current show, and they should be available for reference when planning for future shows.

The fashion show director and staff should be aware of the following categories of expenses:

- Site Rental
- Food or Catering
- Models
- Publicity and Advertising
- Photography
- Technical and Support Staff
- Miscellaneous expenses such as decorations, transportation, hospitality, depreciation of merchandise, insurance, taxes

Site Rental Fees

One of the largest expenses associated with the cost of presenting a fashion show is renting the location where the show will take place. The French couture shows are often held at luxury hotels in Paris. The Grand Hotel in Paris costs 50,000 francs or approximately $8,707 to rent space for a major fashion show. A charitable organization may ask for reduced or waived rental rates. Members of such groups must realize that hotels, restaurants and caterers are often asked for such gratuities. These companies are in business to make a profit, but some may be willing to throw in amenities to benefit the cause or charity.

Realistically most groups whether they are nonprofit or profit making organizations will have to lease the space for the event. A nonprofit organization has 501 c3 status as designated by the Internal Revenue Service. In order to be incorporated as a **nonprofit organization** the organization must have published articles of incorporation and include a board of directors. Additionally, no officer or staff member of the organization may make personal gain from the organization, and there must be no stockholders. All money earned by the organization is returned to the organization. A nonprofit organization may sell tickets and/or ask for donations. The money received may be used for operational expenses or charitable causes.

Costs for the location rental must include the time to set up the facility, present the fashion show, serve refreshments, and clean up. Some of the activities such as room set up and clean up may be handled by the staff at the location. Depending upon the room and facilities these activities may require outside help. Refreshments may be included in the room rental or an outside caterer may be used.

If a rehearsal is required, the estimated cost of using a rehearsal room or renting the site of the actual fashion show must be included in the expenses. If it is not possible to use the contracted space for a rehearsal, another room may be used for planning choreography and practicing the show. Costs for renting all meeting rooms must be added to the budget.

One of the first questions the hotel's sales or marketing director will ask is about the date of the show. The season, day of week, and time of day will impact the price for the room. During the busy seasons such as Thanksgiving through New Year's Eve and the traditional wedding period, hotel banquet rooms are solidly booked, as much as a year in advance. Saturday nights are more expensive than weeknights. Evenings are more costly than day times. The show planners should keep in mind that a hotel sales director may not suggest alternatives if the date for the show has already been established.

If a meal is served in one room while the show is presented in another meeting room, there will be additional charges for the use of two rooms. The hotel representative and show producers must consider where the models will change. One possibility is to use an adjacent meeting room. Another prospect is to use nearby hotel rooms. Costs for these services must be factored into the budget. Some hotels may be willing to waive the rental of the room if specified food and beverage expenditures are met. One rule of thumb used by a national hotel chain requires spending one and one-half times the cost of the room rental on food and beverages for the elimination of separate room rental charges. The fashion show planners should expect to pay a deposit for the hotel services.

Food or Catering Fees

There are two factors to be evaluated in relationship to food service budgets. Food and beverages to be served to the audience must be a foremost concern. However, it may be necessary to provide refreshments to the crew during rehearsal, set up and/or clean up. This would be an appropriate gesture if many of the people participating in the activity are volunteers. Union rules may require serving food to union members dependent upon the amount of time involved.

While an actual contract most likely will be negotiated, at minimum the fashion show staff should expect a written estimate regarding services. Most likely a deposit or prepayment may be required.

Model Fees

The expense of hiring professional models varies from one city to another. Customarily, models are paid on an hourly basis and will include their time at fittings, rehearsals, and the show. Top international models may demand very high salaries. Fees for models at French couture shows start at 6,000 francs or $1,044. A star name may receive as much as 30,000 francs or $5,224. According to *Women's Wear Daily* top models are paid a minimum of $500 an hour for photo shoots. Well-known fashion model celebrities such as Linda Evangelista, Christy Turlington, and Naomi Campbell working through such agencies as Eileen Ford or Elite may be paid as much as $10,000 a day for runway modeling during the presentation of the designer collections.

Models in large markets such as Los Angeles and New York would earn from $600 to $750 an hour for the show. Models working in cities such as San Diego and Phoenix may earn $35 to $50 per hour for fittings and rehearsals, and $75 to $100 for the actual show. Top models known for their photographic work will demand higher fees than runway models. Swimwear and lingerie models will also demand higher rates. Since amateur models are often used for retail or civic shows, it may be appropriate to offer a gift, discount or a gift certificate. The discount will be included as part of the store's markdown allocation and not the fashion show budget. Costs for any gifts or flowers presented to amateur models, however, should be considered as part of the fashion show budget.

Figure 4-2
List of Fashion Show
Expenses

POSSIBLE EXPENSES

1. Rent
   A. Show
   B. Rehearsal
2. Meals
   A. Set up/Rehearsal
   B. Refreshments for Show
3. Ushers
4. Gratuities
   A. Coat Room
   B. Rest Room
   C. Other
5. Models
   A. Fittings
   B. Rehearsal
   C. Show
6. Advertising and Publicity
   A. Invitations
      1) Design
      2) Printing
      3) Mailing
   B. Posters/Programs
   C. Tickets
   D. Photographs
   E. Broadcast Production Radio/TV
   F. Buying Media Time
   G. Press Release/Press Kit
7. Technical Aspects
   A. Photography/Video
   B. Lighting and Electricians
   C. Stage/Runway
      1) Runway Construction
      2) Props
      3) Painting
      4) Carpenters
   D. Public Address System
   E. Music
8. Behind the Scenes Crew
   A. Hair
   B. Makeup
   C. Dressers
   D. Alterations/Pressing
   E. Security
9. Transportation
   A. Clothing
   B. Equipment
   C. Celebrities
10. Hospitality
    A. Celebrities
    B. Guests
11. Depreciation of Merchandise
    A. Alterations
    B. Pressing
    C. Damage
    D. Shortage
12. Insurance
13. Taxes

Publicity and Advertising

Activities relating to publicity and advertising should be included in the budget, including all duties from designing and producing to distributing these materials. Invitations, posters, programs, and tickets need to be designed and printed; invitations need to be mailed or printed in a newspaper or magazine. If tickets are used, there is a cost of buying printed coupons or designing special personalized tickets. The costs for all of these materials must be included in the budget.

To project a consistent look and prevent duplication of the printer's set up costs, one printer can print invitations, posters, programs, and tickets. Also a printer may prefer to bid on a package rather than individual items. Printing costs are determined by the types of services required. Each service increases the cost. There is a cost involved if the size of any artwork needs to be enlarged or reduced to fit on the different size products. Basic black ink is the least expensive color to reproduce. Colored inks and the use of multiple colors are more costly. The type, weight, and color of paper will impact the overall printing cost.

Advertising must include the cost of creative production which involves any artwork, graphic design or layout for print materials. It also involves any photography, models, filming or videotaping, or studio rental. The creation of press releases and press kits may be the responsibility of someone working for the firm producing the show or an outside press agent. These costs of developing press releases, photographs used in the press materials, and any additional materials used to publicize the event must be incorporated into the budget.

If advertising plans include buying spots on radio or television, the cost of producing the commercial becomes a budget item. Buying space in the newspaper or magazine must also be added to budget costs.

Photography

Photography expenses will need to be considered as part of the budget. The fashion show staff will need to determine the type of photography required. The staff may wish to include a photograph rather than artwork for invitations and advertising purposes. This would require hiring a photographer and model prior to the show far enough in advance to allow time for printing.

A photographic record of the show may be desired. Expenses relating to hiring the photographer and supplies would need to be figured into the budget. Supplies might encompass such things as film, paper, processing, and equipment. Press photographers from a newspaper or magazine are sent by their employers to record the event for their medium. Since press photographers are guests and often the target for fashion show publicity, their fees are not included in the budget.

Technical Staff

Salaries for any people hired to perform technical aspects of the show are also part of the budget. Examples of such technical staff include the carpenters hired to build, set up and paint the stage, runway, backdrops or props. The services of electricians who work on the lighting and public address system may be needed. Musicians, recording personnel or disk jockeys may be hired to provide the essential mood creating background music.

Support Staff

The support staff includes all of the behind the scenes personnel who facilitate the smooth and professional appearance of the show. These people are typically the unsung heros of the show. The budget must cover the expenses for the hair stylists, makeup artists, dressers, alterations and pressing people, and security. For charity shows many of these indispensable participants may be volunteers.

Hosts and Ushers The need for people in charge of greeting and directing the audience to their seats increases as the show gets larger and more complex. Members of professional or charitable organizations may serve as volunteers for charity shows. Commercial events may need to hire people or use company employees to help seat the audience.

Members of the audience will be impressed with the organization presenting the show when guests are handled courteously and professionally. Hosts or ushers may act as greeters. The hosts should have a detailed list of guests for shows that require reservations. Hosts and ushers then direct guests to refreshments and seats. Having prearranged seating makes the guests feel welcome.

Gratuities Gratuities are the cash tips given to service people such as waiters or waitresses, attendants in the coat check and rest rooms. Tips may be included in the cost to the hotel, restaurant or caterer and are negotiated at the time the location and services are reserved.

Miscellaneous Expenses

Decorations Decorations of the physical facilities may be limited to the stage and runway set up. More elaborate scenes may include floral arrangements or specialized table settings. Adornment of the room is determined by the type of show, location, audience, and budget allocation. A fashion show with a nautical theme could include miniature ships and red, white and blue table accessories. A southwestern theme could be decorated with coyotes, cactus, conchas and brightly colored textiles.

Ideas for ornamentation are limitless. The theme of the show can be greatly enhanced through decorative elements. Charitable organizations may use table centerpieces as additional fund-raisers by holding a raffle for these elements. The only constraint for decorating are budgetary limitations.

Transportation Transportation costs cannot be omitted from the budget. Clothing may have to be moved from the store or manufacturer to the location of the show. Equipment such as runways, rolling racks, steamers, and furniture may have to be relocated. Transportation of celebrities from another city or within the city may also have to be considered. Hiring a limousine for ground transportation may be necessary.

Hospitality Special arrangements for housing, food or entertainment may be necessary for special guests. A name designer may be brought to a city to meet potential customers at a retail store or for a benefit. The designer may request the participation of his or her favorite models. Additional personnel such as a fashion show coordinator from the designer's staff may travel with the designer to coordinate activities with the local retail store promoting the designer's appearance. Senior executives of the retail company may arrive from other parts of the country. Hotel rooms, meals and transit must be provided for out of town event participants. Any special activities before or after the fashion show for patrons of an organization must be included in the budget.

FASHION SHOW BUDGET

Name of Show_____

Date_____

Location_____

Time_____

	Planned	Actual
REVENUES		
Ticket Sales Qty___ X $___	_____	_____
Vendor Coop Money	_____	_____
EXPENSES		
Physical Facilities		
Room Rental	_____	_____
Chairs	_____	_____
Tables	_____	_____
Food Service	_____	_____
Decorations/Flowers	_____	_____
Stage Set	_____	_____
Runway	_____	_____
Public Address System	_____	_____
Lighting	_____	_____
Technicians & Equipment		
Music	_____	_____
Electrician	_____	_____
Show Photographer	_____	_____
Video Crew	_____	_____
Makeup	_____	_____
Hair Stylist	_____	_____
Show Personnel		
Models	_____	_____
Dressers	_____	_____
Cue People	_____	_____
Transportation Staff	_____	_____
Hosts/Ushers	_____	_____
Publicity & Advertising		
Publicity Materials	_____	_____
Photography	_____	_____
Press Release/Kit	_____	_____
Invitations	_____	_____
Tickets	_____	_____
Programs	_____	_____
Advertising	_____	_____
Creative Production	_____	_____
Media Time/Space	_____	_____
Merchandise		
Damages/Repairs	_____	_____
Lost/Stolen	_____	_____
Insurance	_____	_____
Security	_____	_____
Hospitality		
Celebrity/Guest	_____	_____
Transportation	_____	_____
Hotel Room	_____	_____
Entertainment	_____	_____
Gratuities	_____	_____
Taxes	_____	_____
Emergency Reserve	_____	_____

Figure 4-3

Fashion Show

Budget Form

Depreciation of Merchandise Although great care should be taken in preserving the condition of the garments and accessories, sometimes items break, seams fail or merchandise is missing after the show. Costs of replacing or reconditioning merchandise to its original shape is another item that should be included in the budget.

Insurance The value of the merchandise may require purchasing insurance to guarantee the product in case of theft or damage. Insurance may be needed for such high cost items as jewelry, furs or designer clothes. The cost of the insurance becomes part of the budget.

Taxes Depending upon the geographic location, it may be necessary to be taxed for various services. Taxes may be as high as eight percent in some locations, which can greatly add to the expenses of doing a fashion show.

Often the excitement and enthusiasm of a fashion show overshadow the details necessary to produce a successful show. One such detail that cannot be ignored is the budget. The recession of the 1990s has caused fashion show producers to plan better budgets. Frivolous fashion presentations seem out of place as consumers keep a closer eye on their personal budgets.

Controlling costs will add to the profit if the show is intended to make a profit. Accurately projecting ticket sales will enable fashion show planners to set realistic expectations for spending money on such things as site and model fees, hospitality and staging expenses. In evaluating the success of a show, fashion directors and retail executives will always want to know if the show was within the budgetary limits set prior to the show. If the show comes within budget the executives are more likely to look favorably on the promotion and be responsive to future fashion productions.

KEY FASHION SHOW TERMS

all-one-can-afford method	budgetary process	promotional plan
bottom-up method	fashion show plan	top-down method
budget	nonprofit organization	

ADDITIONAL READINGS

1. Corinth, *Fashion Showmanship* (1970): a budget is essential (pp 89-92).

2. Guerin, *Creative Fashion Presentations* (1987): fashion show budget proposal (pp 156-159).

5

Publicity and Advertising

S ales promotion is any activity that is used to communicate information about goods, services, or ideas to influence sales or acceptance by an intended audience in the form of written and/or oral communications. Typical sales promotion activities involve fashion shows, personal selling, visual merchandising, special events, public relations, publicity and advertising. **Sales promotion** may be **institutional**—enhancing store image, or **promotional**—selling specific products.

Personal selling is the direct interaction between the customer and the seller with the purpose of making a sale. It is one of the most successful forms of sales promotion. It enables the salesperson to promote the characteristics of the product and overcome any objections by the customer. Some customers see this personal attention as validating their selection of a product. **Visual merchandising** is the physical presentation of products in a nonpersonal approach. This may include window, interior, or remote displays.

Special events are activities sponsored by retailers to attract customers to their store while creating goodwill. The range of these activities includes large scale events such as storewide promotions and simple showings of isolated products. Store image is differentiated through execution of special events. It is becoming more important as a device to draw customers into the store during off peak selling seasons. Fashion shows may be a part of a special event.

Public relations (PR) is the interrelationship between service providers and the public as it relates to the image of the organization through all levels of communication. PR as it is also known, may analyze public opinion and create programs to improve relationships with the public. **Publicity** is non-paid, un-sponsored information delivered at the discretion of the media. **Advertising** is information paid for and controlled by the sponsoring organization.

Visual merchandising and personal selling are important forms of sales promotion, however, fashion shows rarely depend upon these activities to inform the public about upcoming

Marc Jacobs looks
exuberant at the end of
his show. (*WWD*)

shows and special events. The forms of sales promotion most often used in fashion show production are public relations, publicity, and advertising. All fashion shows, regardless of the kind or size, require promotion to create interest in the show, and attract an audience.

PUBLICITY

Publicity is non-paid, un-sponsored information delivered at the discretion of the media, initiated by the party seeking to tell others about the event. The organization informs the media of the event through publicity; the media in turn informs the public of the event. It is consequently important to present the information to the media in a very newsworthy manner so that the news value of the event will be passed to the audience. Publicity is run at the discretion of the editor or program director. Editors must read many press releases every day and determine which if any will be run in the newspaper. If the day is extremely full of local or national news, publicity spots get pushed to the next day or omitted completely.

Publicity is released to the public through **press releases**, **press photographs**, or **press shows**. Common outlets for sending press releases include daily newspapers and Sunday editions, community weekly newspapers, trade newspapers, and magazines; consumer, women's interest, home and living, and fashion sections. Articles and photographs generated by press releases and photographs often appear in the fashion, women's, or community sections of local newspapers or magazines or broadcast during hours which the intended audiences are more likely to listen. Press shows are private showings for press delivered before the public is allowed to view the fashions.

Press Releases

A **press release** is a written article on a newsworthy event, sent to editors or news directors for publication or broadcast in the media. The information includes all the details about the event, and is written to gain the attention of an editor or the news director. If the editor or news director finds the event to be interesting they will then run the narrative in their media.

To gain the editor's or news director's interest the press release should not be long winded. Press releases are usually limited to one or two pages. Longer press releases become redundant and lose the attention of the reader. Press releases should always be hand-delivered or mailed first class.

Press releases are not specific to fashion show publicity. Variations of style may occur, but they follow a standard form and are used by any organization or individual wishing to publicize an event.

Guidelines for Press Releases   When writing a press release the following guidelines should be used to help facilitate the information being published in printed media. A press release should not be handwritten. Use a typewriter or word-processor and submit copy on $8\frac{1}{2}$ x 11 inch, white paper (non-transparent)—using only one side of the page. The copy should be double-spaced with left and right margins at least one inch, and top and bottom margins at least two inches. Margins are wide to allow for editing or revisions from the editor. The actual copy of the release should start approximately halfway down the page. Copy is the actual material to be printed in the media, excluding headings and other material such as the release date or special to information used only by the editor. Paragraph openings should be indented five spaces with an extra line space added to the double spacing between paragraphs. If the press release is more than one page, all the pages after the first page should be numbered in the upper right-hand corner and include a two- or three-word heading, repeating important words from the headline, in the upper left-hand corner. The word "more" should be used at the bottom of any page where copy is continued. Never break a paragraph from one page to another. At the conclusion of the press release the symbol #### appears in the center at the bottom of the page.

The press release should include the following information. The company name and address should be typed in the upper left-hand corner followed by the contact person and phone number for the event. If letterhead stationery is used, the company name and address can be omitted. The contact person may be the show coordinator or the publicity chair, whoever wrote the press release. An individual should not be listed as the contact person unless he or she is informed about the event. A common error is to list organization presidents who are so far removed from the actual workings of the event that they can provide little information to a caller. A release date should be included to inform the editor when the release should run in the media. Editors prefer an actual date to the commonly used statement "for immediate release." An optional statement may be included to notify the editor of others who will receive the release. "Exclusive to" indicates that the press release is written to that publication only and will not be delivered to any other publication. "Special to" indicates that the press release is written for a specific publication.

The headline, lead, and amplification should also be included in the press release. The headline should be typed, centered, all in upper case letters and underlined, placed approximately one third down the page. The headline should be the title of the release including the news value of the story, using an action verb. It is not necessarily the title the publisher will use for the story.

Figure 5-1

All the elements of a press release are used to announce a local charity fashion show.

```
Fashion Merchandising          For Immediate Release
School of Art & Design

Box 6030
Northern Arizona University

Kris Swanson
304A School of Art & Design
(602) 523-4216

            FASHION MERCHANDISING STUDENTS PRESENT
                    ANNUAL FASHION SHOW

     Students of Fashion Merchandising at Northern
Arizona University are presenting their annual spring
fashion show "So Many Clothes, So Little Time", April
5, 1992 at 7:30 P.M. at the Carriage House at Riordan
State Park. Tickets for the limited seats can be pur-
chased for $5.00 adults and $4.00 students by calling
773-5872. Proceeds will go to the Cystic Fibrosis
Foundation.
     Local merchants will provide the clothing and
accessories which will be presented in a runway style
show. The show is being presented by students
enrolled in Fashion Promotion and Coordination taught
by Kristen Swanson of the Fashion Merchandising area.
Students are responsible for models, music, merchan-
dise, and other elements of the show. For information
call Kris Swanson at 523-4216 in the School of Art &
Design at Northern Arizona University. For tickets
call 773-5872.
                         ####
```

The lead is the most important part of the press release. It is one or two sentences that summarize the news including who, what, where, when, and why of the event.

The amplification follows the lead and provides additional information and facts about the event. Amplification may be one or several paragraphs always written in diminishing order of importance. There is limited space available to an editor and he or she may chose to omit copy within the press release. It is imperative to list the most important information first.

Press releases should be written objectively, not subjectively, from a third person point of view. Do not use I, we, or you when writing the release. The writer should not show biased interest in the event by using opinionated words when describing the event. Fill the press release with facts not opinions. It is important to follow the correct format so the press release will not be discarded before the content is read.

Press Photographs

Press photographs are photographs prepared specifically for use in print media to accompany press releases or to be included in a press kit. Some organizations and publications use illustrations but this is not common for fashion shows. Just as press releases are presented in a standard form so are press photographs. It may be wise to ask the editors of the publications if they prefer a different format from the standard format described below and if the publication would provide a staff photographer to prepare the photography. Although the same press release may be sent to the several publications, press photographs must be exclusive to each publication. The same photograph should not be sent to more than one publication.

Guidelines for Press Photographs Photographs should be either 8 x 10 inch or 5 x 7 inch glossy stock in black and white only. A 4 x 5 inch photo may be used for portraits only. The fashions or the models should be emphasized; avoid busy backgrounds. Too much activity in the background will draw attention from the subject.

Handle photographs carefully so as not to leave any fingerprints on the photos. Identify each photograph on the back with a felt-tip pen in case they are separated from the press release or caption. Do not use a ball-point pen.

All press photographs should be accompanied by a caption, even if they are sent with a press release. The caption should be typed with the same identification information as the press release; company name, address, contact person, phone and fax number. Five or six lines are sufficient for a caption. People should always be identified left to right including full names, titles, and firm affiliations. A model release should be obtained from all models or individuals in the photographs. All syndicated or stock photographs must be credited. Other photographs may be credited as required by the publication. Headlines are not necessary but may be used to enhance the photograph. Captions should be written just as for press releases, in the third person, using objective not subjective language. Captions should be attached to the bottom of the back side of the photograph with rubber cement.

The press release and photographs should be sent to the media to be published as close to the event as possible. The publicity writer must give plenty of time to the editor to review the materials. They should be delivered no later than two weeks before the event is staged. Successful publicity is often delivered to the editor a full month before the event is held.

KARL LAGERFELD
144 AVENUE DES CHAMPS ELYSEES
75008 - PARIS
TEL. : 43.59.57.50

PRINTEMPS - ETE 1991

VESTE LEGEREMENT CINTREE EN NATTE DE
COTON MARINE A DOUBLE COLSUR BLOUSE
COMBINAISON ET COLLANT CORSAIRE.

NAVY BLUE COTION BASKETWEAVE FITTED
JACKET, DOUBLE COLLAR OVER TUNIC AN
CAPRI LEGGINGS.

COIFFURE : GERALD POUR ALEXANDRE DE PARIS
MAQUILLAGE : PIERRE MARIE HUMEAU

MENTION OBLIGATOIRE : KARL LAGERFELD
OBLIGATORY MENTION : KARL LAGERFELD

EKTA SUR DEMANDE
EKTA ON REQUEST

PHOTOGRAPHE : KARL LAGERFELD

The caption for a press photo uses the same basic information and format as the press release. (Courtesy of Karl Lagerfeld.)

Press Kits

If the event is of extreme importance the press release and photographs may be combined with additional material and presented in a press kit. A press kit is a collection of materials delivered or mailed to the press in a folder with inside pockets to hold the contents. The contents include press releases, news stories, feature stories, fact sheets, photographs with captions, biographical or historical information about the event or people involved, and brochures or samples. The folder is usually graphically illustrated to present the theme of the event, reinforcing its importance to impress the editor.

It is important to select the right kind of publicity to match the event being publicized. If the show is very large with great fashion influence the publicity should reach national fashion magazines. If the show is small, raising funds for a local charity, the publicity should be aimed at local publications that reach the public who will be directly affected by the charity.

ADVERTISING

Advertising is information paid for and controlled by the sponsoring organization notifying the public about an event. As long as standards are acceptable for publication or broadcast, advertisements or commercials run as submitted by the sponsoring organization.

Press kit announcing the
Ebony Fashion Fair. (*Ebony*
Fashion Magazine)

To use advertising for a fashion show, sponsors will either buy space in print media or buy time in broadcast media. Advertising can be purchased in newspapers and magazines, or broadcast on television, network or cable, or radio. The cost of advertising is based on specific rates of the publication or network, frequency of the advertisement or commercial, and any special requests of the advertiser. The only way to accurately determine the cost of advertising for a fashion show is to call local media outlets and ask for rates prior to purchasing advertising. Advertising should supplement publicity not replace it. However, press releases should be delivered to all publications and broadcast networks regardless of any planned advertising.

Newspapers

The most common form of advertising for a retail or consumer oriented fashion show is through newspapers. Newspapers reach local audiences most efficiently and are cost effective compared to other forms of publicity such as magazines and broadcast media.

Advertising in newspapers is sold either by an advertising unit or by a standard line rate, the more common advertising unit. The basic rate of a newspaper advertisement entitles the advertiser to a **run-of-paper position (R.O.P. rate)**. This means the advertisement may be run on any page in any position within the paper. If the advertising budget is large enough it may be beneficial to pay a slightly higher rate called a **preferred position** and specify the page or position of the advertisement in the paper. Two examples of the range of advertising rates as of July 1990 are included the: Rocky Mountain News, Denver, Colorado, with a circulation of 364,790 (March, 1990) publishes in tabloid form, 5 columns wide and 14 inches high. A standard advertising unit is 1 column by 1 inch deep selling for $700 daily, $76 Sunday. These are run-of-paper rates but the advertiser may request a section of the paper for the art to run such as in business, sports, community news. Another example is the Arizona Republic/Phoenix Gazette, Phoenix, Arizona, with a circulation of 484,432 (March, 1990) publishes as a standard, 6 columns wide, 21½ inches deep. Their standard advertising unit is 1 column by 1½ inches deep selling for $122.10 daily, $141.40 Sunday. These rates are run-of-paper rates with the preferred position advertising sold.

It is best to call local newspapers and ask what the advertising unit for that newspaper is

Newspaper advertising rates include the city, newspaper, and circulation. Source: Gale Directory of Publications & Broadcast Media, 1992.

CITY	NEWSPAPER	CIRCULATION		ADV.	RATE
Atlanta	Atlanta Constitution	D - Sat- Sun-	329,582 533,306 700,739	SAU	167.44
Boston	Boston Globe	D - Sat- Sun-	516,981 474,977 798,298	SAU	184.25
Boston	Boston Herald	D - Sat- Sun-	351,947 277,530 230,654	BW PCI	10,850 155
Chicago	Chicago Sun Times	D - Sat- Sun-	537,780 361,448 559,093	GLR BW 4C PCI	15.18 10,305 13,205 212.45
Chicago	Chicago Tribune	D - Sat- Sun-	741,345 631,284 1,131,226	SAU	263.00
Los Angeles	Daily News	D - Sat- Sun-	185,736 173,062 202,614	GLR BW 4C PCI	$5.61 10,269 11,469 81.50
Los Angeles	LA Times	D- Sat- Sun-	1,242,864 1,122,221 1,576,425	SAU PCI	325.10 416.00
New York	New York Times	D- Sat- Sun-	1,209,225 951,419 1,762,015	SAU	337.20
Seattle	News/Herald	Pd - Free -	15,946 19,685	GLR BW 4C SAU	.88 1,587.60 1,947.28 12.60
Seattle	Seattle Times	D - Sat- Sun-	237,735 231,930 515,347	BW 4C SAU	13,481.10 16,596.10 99.86

GLR - General Line Rate
BW - One-time Black/White Page
4C - One-time Four Color Page
SAU - Standard Advertising Rate
PCI - Per Column Inch

and request a rate card. Rate cards are the published rates on advertising units and are available to the public. The advertising unit, space designated in column inches, may be slightly discounted from the line rate but may not be available to small space advertisers. Small space advertisers may have to pay according to a line rate which may be higher than the line rate given to a customer buying larger volumes of advertising. Volume advertising may be purchased according to volume inches or time period.

Newspaper advertisements may be created by the publicity chair of the fashion show or by the newspaper advertising department. The layout cost is generally the same regardless of whether the show or newspaper personnel create the advertisement. It is important to ask the newspaper what is preferred and be ready to create the advertisement if necessary. One account executive stated her newspaper prefers whatever works best for the advertiser, and that approximately ninety percent of her clients who had the newspaper staff create the advertisements found the advertisements to be acceptable with only minor changes. An advertising designer stated that on a limited fashion show budget the newspaper should create the advertisement to save costs rather than paying an outside source additional funds to typeset the advertisement. Generally newspapers have advertisements prepared two weeks in advance of when they will be run in the newspaper.

Many newspapers have fashion editors whose exclusive responsibility is fashion. This is the best person to contact at a newspaper regarding fashion show advertising or publicity. The fashion editor often knows the angle from which to direct the publicity or advertising to best expose the event to the public. Small newspapers might not have a fashion editor, but frequently feature or community editors will be the best contacts.

Preparing Newspaper Advertisements   A newspaper advertisement is composed of copy, art, and white space. The reading material within the advertisement is designated as copy. Illustrations or photography are designated as art of the advertisement, and space between the copy and art is designated as white space.

The shape of the white space is determined by the size of the advertisement. The size of the advertisement should be determined by the publicity chair and the newspaper based on the cost of the spot. Review the dimensions of the advertisement to ensure accuracy before preparing the ad. Two points should be considered when planning an advertisement. First, white space, copy, and art in advertisements should balance proportionally. Advertisements with too much white space are considered boring by the reader and advertisements with too little white space are overlooked by the reader because they are hard to read. No rules determine the balance of white space to art or copy but ultimately it should be pleasing to the reader. Secondly, the designer of the advertisement must consider the viewing center of an advertisement. Readers will naturally place the center of the advertisement five-eighths from the bottom. An advertisement should not be divided in equal halves top and bottom, creating a top or bottom heavy spot.

Copy may include one or several of the following components: headline, subheadline, body, slogan, or logo. Headlines attract the attention of the reader and create interest in the advertisement. This may contain the wording "fashion show" or the show theme. Subheadlines are used to further explain the headline. They may inform the reader of the intended audience. Body includes the important details needed in the advertisement, such as the day, date, time, location, and price of the fashion show. The body should further stimulate the reader to want to attend the event. The slogan is usually a catchy phrase which is appealing when spoken or viewed in print. If the theme of the fashion show has not previously been used in the advertisement, it may be used as a slogan. The slogan should be easily remembered by the reader. If the fashion show is produced in cooperation with a retailer or organization the company logo, a copyright protected symbol or phrase, may be incorporated in the advertisement. Repeating a logo in an advertisement creates immediate identification to the reader and increases interest in the event.

Line drawings, photographs, and halftones are considered artwork in the advertisement. A line drawing is created by pen, pencil, brush or crayon, as illustration for a printed advertisement. Photography is the reproduction of prints created by a camera. Halftones are reproduced photographs or drawings using screens to convert the design into a series of dots, making shaded values possible. Artwork must effectively create a visual message promoting the fashion show and attracting the reader's attention. The reader should first be aware of the artwork; the copy should serve to complement the artwork.

Reproduction quality is best achieved in newspapers by using line drawings. Line drawings consist of only lines to create shapes and shading. Halftones rely on tones of watercolor such as crayon, chalk, or pencil to create the illustration. Halftones reproduce better than photographs but require skill beyond the amateur level to achieve the desired effect. Photography is the least desired medium in newspaper advertisements because of the poor reproduction quality of the newsprint. If photography is used, follow the guidelines for press photography stated previously in this chapter. Examine your local newspaper to determine what is used most frequently for publication.

Clip art, prefabricated illustrations, generated on a computer or purchased in clip art books, is quickly becoming popular when creating advertising artwork. Time and expense are reduced by finalizing the artwork in the correct size from the computer before delivering it to the newspaper. Many local businesses now have computers for the general public to use. Check with local copy centers and computer stores for information.

Copy, art, and white space must be arranged within the boundaries of the advertisement—layout. Often the publicity chair will submit rough sketches of a layout to the advertising representative of the newspaper. The representative will in turn have the art department of the newspaper reproduce the rough draft into an advertisement using materials not available to the publicity chair. The reproduction is called a paste-up and returned to the sponsor for review before final production is run. When both the sponsor and the newspaper have approved the advertisement, the newspaper will put the spot into production. Upon final production the newspaper will produce the advertisement and deliver a tear sheet to the sponsor. The tear sheet is the advertisement, torn directly from the newspaper, to show proof of publication to the advertiser. The tear sheet should be saved and included with other items submitted for evaluation after the show.

Depending on the type of fashion show and newspaper it may be advantageous to buy space in the classified section. These sections are often less expensive than other advertising and may have a large readership. If the target audience includes a college age group, classified sections of school newspapers are a good choice for advertising.

Magazines

Magazine advertising is generally used to reach a national market or a specific area through special editions. Advertising in magazines for a fashion show may be best achieved in city or state magazines that inform the local reader of happenings in their own city. National magazines are less frequently used for fashion shows because of their large readership base. Magazines sell space by the page or by a portion of a page based on column inches. An advantage to magazine advertising is the excellent reproduction quality of photography not available in newspapers. However it is more expensive because the paper used is better quality and the photography can be in color.

Timing of advertising in magazines is often more difficult to arrange than that for newspapers. Magazines are usually published monthly so advertising or press releases must be delivered up to six weeks before the event is to occur. Meeting this kind of deadline may be prohibitive, if all the details of the show have not been decided. Magazine and newspaper advertisements are created in the same way.

Network and Cable Television

Television is the most influential type of advertising available and the most expensive. Only the largest fashion show budgets are able to afford television advertising. The costs of television advertising are based on the length of the advertisement—15-, 20-, 30- or 60-second—and the specified time the advertisement will run. Prime time, from 7:00 to 11:00 P.M., will have the highest rates but the most viewers. The rates to advertise on television should be carefully evaluated before deciding on this type of advertising for fashion shows.

To advertise on television the sponsor must buy time as network advertising, spot advertising, or local advertising, local advertisements being the most economical. Network advertising is time bought on one of the three major networks— ABC, CBS, or NBC—during a specified show. The network produces the shows and the commercials, and sends the package to network affiliates. Costs are the greatest for network commercials because they are produced nationally; $70,000 is not uncommon for a network budget for 60-second commercials.

Time bought on independently owned stations is considered spot advertising. Advertising is purchased by quantity and generally run in a specific time frame rather than during a specific show. Commercials on these stations are produced both nationally and locally, and can service a specific geographic area. Spot advertising is less expensive than network advertising but still may range in the thousands of dollars. Check with local independent stations about their production procedures and rates.

Local advertising is time purchased on local television stations by businesses or organizations. Advertising costs at these stations more readily fit into fashion show budgets because the shows are produced in and for the immediate area. If merchandise used in the fashion show is borrowed from a local retailer, it may be wise to ask the retailer to share in the cost of the commercial, since both parties will benefit from the advertising.

One small television station cited rates from $25 to $300 for a 30-second spot. During daytime hours the commercials were between $20 and $40 while prime time advertising ran from $100 to $300. Production time from start to finish when producing a local commercial was approximately two hours according to this source. Some advertisers will participate in creating the commercial while other advertisers leave it to the station. One advertiser produced the photography and selected the music, participating in about 75 percent in the production of the ad. A second retailer only participated by writing copy, contributing approximately 25 percent of the production time. A 30-second commercial should have approximately 70 words and photography should be in the form of videotape if possible. Photographs often loose their appeal in the transition onto video. The sales manager of this small television station cautioned that groups are encouraged to advertise on television but that they should be highly organized with one person making decisions. If the decisions need to be discussed with all the members, too much time is wasted and production engineers may lose their patience.

Public service announcements (PSA's) are television or radio spots run free of charge to charitable organizations to deliver a message about their organization or benefit. PSA's should be considered if the fashion show is of interest to the community. One local station commented that they would run PSA's if the organization was non-profit and the organization was not spending money on advertising in any other media.

Many communities now have local cable stations. Frequently these stations will run local commercials at a cost significantly lower than the local network affiliate. If television or cable commercials are too expensive, deliver press releases to the stations. Public service announcements are always available on the air if the station deems the event newsworthy.

Radio

Radio is considered to be a cost effective medium compared to other broadcast media. Radio advertising is sold in 10-, 20-, 30- and 60-second spots. Portions of shows may also be purchased and sponsored by the advertiser. Prime time is considered drive time in the morning and the evenings, from 6:00 to 9:00 A.M. and from 4:00 to 7:00 P.M. When advertising fashion shows it may be best to use only local or regional radio.

Different fashion show audiences will listen to different radio stations so it is important to match the show to the station. Check with local stations to determine rates.

Radio Commercials Because of the many varieties of radio stations, on-the-air, radio commercials must target specific audiences more than print media. Commercials must be brief but they must get the message across. A 60-second commercial should be limited to 125 words. Shorter commercials should be planned accordingly. Radio commercials can be prepared in two forms: they can be read live on the air, or taped in advanced and played on the air. If the fashion show budget does not include a prepared radio commercial, press releases should be delivered to all radio stations in a community two to four weeks before the event. Like television, PSA's will be broadcast if the event is perceived by the news director as noteworthy.

A promotion coordinator who is considering television or radio advertising should seriously evaluate the use of a professional advertising agency to produce the commercial. Professional agencies have studio space, equipment, and design talent not available to the layperson. Commercials, to be effective, must be of the highest quality to retain listeners.

```
CLIENT: NAU Fashion Merchandising          LENGTH: 30 seconds
SERVICE ANNOUNCEMENT:              Annual Spring Fashion Show

TITLE: So Many Clothes, So Little Time
_____

RISE AND SHINE Harry Belafonte
MUSIC OF FASHION SHOW FADES AS
ANNOUNCER STARTS TO SPEAK
ANNOUNCER
          Fashion Merchandising students at Northern Arizona
          University are presenting their annual spring fashion
          show "So Many Clothes, So Little Time", April 5,
          1992 at 7:30 P.M. at the Carriage House at Riordan
          State Park. Tickets for the limited seats can be
          purchased for $5.00 adults and $4.00 students by
          calling 773-5872. Proceeds will go to the Cystic
          Fibrosis Foundation. Local merchants will provide
          the clothing and accessories which will be presented
          in a runway style show.
MUSIC UP—
          Don't miss this opportunity to see the exciting new
          fashions for this spring and help out the Cystic
          Fibrosis Foundation. See you there!
```

Figure 5-4

Script for a 60-second radio spot announcing a local charity fashion show.

Non-broadcast or Print Media

Signage, posters, direct mail, and transit media such as billboards and bus benches may serve as acceptable media for advertising. These valuable forms of promotion are not considered to be broadcast or print media, despite the fact that transit media is actually printed material.

Direct Mail Probably the easiest type of advertising to use for a fashion show is **direct mail advertising**, or **direct advertising**. Direct mail advertising is advertising sent through the mail. Materials left on the tops of counters or desks for people to pick up are direct advertising. Costs of direct mail or direct advertising are determined by printing and mailing costs. These costs are usually better accommodated by a fashion show budget than other types of advertising. Two common forms of direct mail include flyers and written invitations. Flyers sent through the mail are excellent for reaching general audiences. Audiences at mall shows may be targeted with posters, while members of organizations may better appreciate written invitations.

The price of postage must be analyzed when evaluating the advertising sales plan. Mailing lists are an important tool when using direct-mail advertising. Membership lists of organizations and customer lists of retailers should be used whenever possible to create a larger audience.

Invitations If the target market is well defined, such as a retail store's mailing list, invitations are an excellent way to inform the audience of the show. If the location of the

This formal engraved invitation for the Albert Nipon fashion show was sent to special customers.

show is small, invitations with an RSVP will control the size of the audience. Invitations and direct mail should include the design or logo for the show as well as the following information: show title which should reflect the type of show it is, day, date, time, location, and sponsoring group. Information regarding tickets and prices should be stated along with other information such as door prizes and refreshments if any. Always state the information as simply and specifically as possible carefully avoiding too many words. If invitations are used as tickets, they should be numbered. This helps in reserve seating and in the show evaluation after the event. Invitations should be sent two weeks in advance of the event.

Signage and Posters   Another type of advertising closely related to direct advertising is signage and posters. Posters (8½" x 14" or 11" x 17") can be read easily and quickly from a distance, promoting a product or event. Signage is in-store visual identification. Signage and posters can be placed at the store entrance or near escalators.

Keep in mind that all signage and posters must attract the attention of the reader in order to be effective. Signage must be neat and legible from a distance. Handwritten posters tend to wash out words from a distance. Computer-generated signs are now becoming popular because of legibility and diversity in software for sign making. Although not a strong type of advertising for large retail operations, signage can be very effective to advertise fashion shows at the local level, such as for community shows.

As with direct mail, posters can often be printed in bulk for an inexpensive rate and distributed to a large local population or folded in quarters and mailed. Prices vary but generally work well in a fashion show budget.

Transit Media   Billboards, above-the-seat subway or bus signage, signage on bus stop benches or other outside locations which commuters pass are some examples of transit media.

Bus benches are becoming the most popular form of transit advertising because they are relatively inexpensive. According to Carol Robins, vice president of the National Bench Advertising Association, bus benches cost between $50 and $90 and billboards can cost anywhere from $500 to $18,000. Coast United is the largest owner of bus benches in the country, controlling 22,000 bus benches in California alone. This association may be a good source to start researching transit media as a form of advertising for a fashion show.

The cost of this type of advertising is based on the size of the space, location of space, and length of time the advertisement will run. A fashion show produced by fashion students at Colorado State University, Fort Collins, Colorado, was effectively advertised on a billboard on a major crossroad, close to the university. Rates and effectiveness will vary from city to city.

Since many people are unfamiliar with transit media, the following list of tips should help the unfamiliar be more comfortable with this type of advertising.

1. The advertisement must be readable by people driving 55 mph with a three-second read time.
2. The design must be very simple and uncluttered.
3. Condensed script which may blur from a distance should not be used.
4. Too much white and gray, and other similar color combinations may blend from a distance.

5. Outdoor transit advertising has a larger discrepancy rate between what is purchased and what is provided than other forms of media, therefore the agreement should be confirmed in writing.

It is important to select the right type of advertising to get the most viewers for the dollars while attracting the right target market. Monies spent on publicity and advertising should always be carefully planned for before they are spent.

DIFFERENCES BETWEEN PUBLICITY AND ADVERTISING

Publicity should always be used; advertising should be used if the show budget is large enough to afford this type of promotion. Because publicity is non-paid promotion it requires careful planning to ensure an editor or program director will choose to publish or broadcast the information. Advertising is paid for, with the guarantee that it will run, but is often too expensive to be used extensively.

Costs

Both publicity and advertising should be budgeted. Publications and networks have set costs for advertising based on the type of media, geographic location, and size of circulation or listening audience. Rate costs, the cost of advertising during a specified period of time in a specified media, will also vary greatly depending on the quarter of the year in which the advertising is purchased. Rate costs differ when purchased closer to the show time, when deadlines are more critical. Ideally, advertising should be purchased in the first quarter of the year when rates are the lowest. Since most of the business in retail occurs in the last quarter of the year, the rates from August through December will be the most expensive.

Publicity, although it is non-paid, has costs associated with production and must not be considered free advertising. Printing, typesetting, postage, and other production costs should always be considered when determining the budget for publicity.

THE PROMOTION COORDINATOR

Although the show coordinator has the ultimate responsibility for promoting the show, it can be a very time-consuming activity. When time is critical the task of promotion should be delegated to a committee with the single responsibility of show promotion or to an individual—the promotion coordinator. The promotion coordinator is responsible for the creation and distribution of promotional materials required for the show including the preparation of press releases, press photographs, commercials, signage, and other forms of promotion. The promotion coordinator will also perform public relations activities. This person must be knowledgeable about publicity and advertising and be willing to ask questions of the media advertising representatives. It is critical to select the most appropriate type of advertising for the intended fashion show rather than the least expensive or easiest method of production. At times advertising representatives are more interested in selling advertising than providing advice as to the most appropriate advertising for the intended event. Always be informed before contacting the advertising representative.

The promotion coordinator may generate a media list to use when planning print or broadcast promotions. A media list is a local and/or regional list of media which might be used to publicize an event. It includes all newspapers and magazines—daily, weekly, and monthly; television networks—local and independent; radio stations—all music categories, AM and FM; billboards and bus media, and any other local media that may publicize the event.

Other Responsibilities of the Promotion Coordinator

Since promotion deals with print material and media, other responsibilities for the promotion coordinator include planning tickets and ticket sales and planning and printing programs as well as coordinating extras such as door prizes, giveaways, and refreshments which might be part of the show.

Tickets   Sending out invitations is one way to control the number of attendees. A second way to monitor the audience is to sell tickets. As with invitations, tickets can be used to reserve seats and evaluate the show. They are a reminder to the holder of the event. Tickets can also generate a mailing list for future shows if there is room for the attendees to write in their names and addresses and the tickets are collected. Tickets can be prepared with a perforated section so part of the ticket can be returned and part held by the audience member. These tickets are used when door prizes are given at the show.

It is always an issue whether to sell or give away tickets. There are advantages to both free and sponsored shows. Shows free to the public are often common in retail stores. The cost of producing the show is usually recovered in retail sales after the show. With free shows many tickets are distributed with attendance ranging from a very low to a very high percentage of the total tickets distributed. Response rates increase if the show is specialized such as a bridal show, and if tickets must be picked up at a certain location, such as at the information booth of the retail mall.

A minimal charge lends a degree of exclusivity to the show, causing it to have greater importance to the ticket holder. When tickets are sold, the number of tickets distributed will be lower but the percentage rate for those who attend will be greater. Plan for a 15 percent no-show and print that many extra tickets. Tickets can be printed at local print shops or purchased in rolls at stationery or office supply stores. If the show is being produced at an auditorium or a theater, the cost of printing the tickets may be part of the rental fee. Check with the management; do not assume the cost of the tickets is included.

Tickets should be carefully proofread to make sure day, date, time, and location are correctly printed. When these errors are not caught in time, the fashion show staff must either hand mark the tickets or additional money must be spent to reprint them. If reserved seating is used then tickets must be marked with the seat number. Tickets can be designed to complement the rest of the printed material, contributing to a well-coordinated package.

Programs   Printed programs serve as an outline or guide of the merchandise being presented. Programs may or may not be used depending on the type of show. Mall shows with

Programs are distributed to guests as they arrive to provide information about the show and merchandise.

GLAMOUR IN SYNC

THE BRIGHT SIDE

1. Liz & Co. orange quilted anorak jacket, orange fuchsia striped top and fuchsia knit pants
2. Liz & Co. purple/lime quilted jacket, striped t-top and purple knit pants
3. Liz & Co. multi-color oversized sweater over purple turtleneck and orange leggings
4. Adrienne Vittadini sport multi-color sweater, fuchsia turtleneck by Liz & Co. and black knit pants
5. Lime crochet sweater by One Step Up over Guess black jeans
6. Orange crochet sweater by One Step Up and Guess black jeans
7. Axiom fuchsia handknit sweater, turquoise turtleneck and black stirrup pants
8. Axiom emerald hand knit sweater, purple turtleneck and black stirrup pants
9. Liz Claiborne yellow hand knit sweater, jade turtleneck and black stirrup pants
10. Axiom purple handknit sweater, red turtleneck and black stirrup pants
11. Starting Point blue suede baseball jacket over Guess black corduroy skirt and jade cotton turtleneck
12. Starting Point green suede over blue cotton turtleneck over black Guess corduroy skirt
13. Liz Claiborne red double breasted blazer over black and red striped Liz Claiborne sweater with black stirrup pants
14. Liz Claiborne black cardigan sweater over yellow turtleneck and black stirrup pants
15. Liz Claiborne black and white houndstooth jacket over yellow blouse and black skirt
16. Liz Claiborne red shawl collar sweater over cream crewneck sweater and black skirt

COUNTRY ROADS

17. Outerbound brown suede fringed jacket over Guess brown corduroy jeans
18. Outerbound hunter green suede fringed jacket over Jordache stretch green jeans
19. Down filled jacket with suede appliques by Gallery
20. Liz Claiborne camel color outerwear jackets with navy plaid cotton shirt and white cotton long sleeve tee with Liz Claiborne jeans
21. Liz Claiborne denim bomber over navy Lizwear sweater and light blue and navy striped cotton tee with denim jeans
22. Jones denim anorak with cinched waist over Liz Claiborne, crewneck knit and button up blue striped shirt with Jones straight jean skirt
23. Oui Int'l washed jean jacket with brown suede insets over Lizwear chambray print shirt and Lizsport vest with Lizwear jeans
24. Brown suede bomber jacket over plaid Liz Claiborne cotton blouse with Liz Claiborne knit sweater vest with Calvin Klein jeans
25. Dana Buchman olive print cardigan over red scarf tie, olive suede skirt by Design Assets
26. Liz Claiborne olive tweed blazer over Liz Claiborne maroon knit vest with paisley blouse and Design Assets brown suede skirt
27. Liz Claiborne olive print cardigan over maroon cotton turtleneck with olive corduroy shorts
28. Ellen Tracy taupe mock turtleneck with Liz & Co. print vest with Esprit red corduroy shorts
29. Esprit olive wool jacket over ivory shirt and brown suede shorts
30. Olive wool blazer by Esprit over olive shirt, taupe cardigan sweater and plaid pleated skirt
31. Esprit henna colored wool full length coat over mustard turtleneck and plaid vest with Liz Claiborne cuffed pants in corduroy

BROADWAY SOUTHWEST

audiences filtering in and out may not need programs. Programs for special event shows may help the audience keep track of the garments they intend to try on after the show.

In most cases, the program will list the garments in show order with a brief description of each ensemble. Model's names may or may not be used in the program, depending upon the type of show. Price is seldom listed unless the audience is very budget minded. Most people will investigate the garments they like regardless of price. Programs may also acknowledge the designers, manufacturers, retailers or staff who volunteered their help to produce the show. This not only thanks those people who helped, it provides some publicity for businesses such as printers, photographers, hair stylists, cosmeticians, or technicians that have provided assistance. It can also serve to reinforce the charity and group sponsoring the show.

As with all printed materials, the design of the programs should carry through the theme established, not detract from the show. It is better to have no program than a program which was slapped together at the last minute.

Advertising space may be sold in programs. Rates are usually determined by the sponsoring organization. This is a way to increase profits of the show or cover advertising expenses.

Door Prizes and Giveaways Door prizes and giveaways are used to build interest in the show and thank the audience for attending. Depending on the type of show, few or many of these presents may be used.

Door prizes are gifts, given to selected members of the audience as an acknowledgment for purchasing a ticket. Prizes may be a large item such as a fur coat or luxury vacation. They may be small items such as watches, cosmetics or accessories. The actual products may be donated by manufacturers, retailers or service providers such as manicurists and beauticians. Usually the prizes are awarded at intermission or after the show and are related to the merchandise or organizations holding the event. It is rewarding when the door-prize winner has been an enthusiastic audience member during the show. Show producers should not advertise a door prize and then forget to give it away. Audience members may have come specifically for the

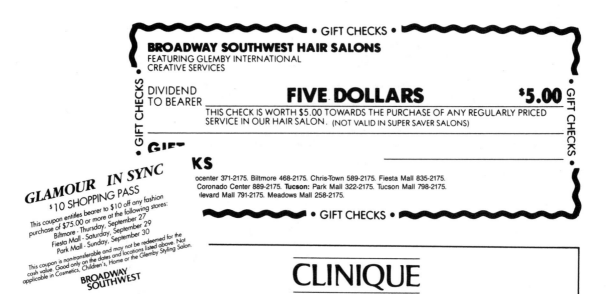

Giveaways may take the form of samples, gift certificates or store services and may be included in a packet with the program.

drawing and may feel cheated if the prize is not awarded.

Giveaways include any token given to every audience member. A very common give-away item is a cosmetic or perfume sample. Pens or pencils to mark the programs or other promotional items may also be used. Coupons offering discounts or free gifts when presented at a participating merchant are customary giveaways. These items can be placed on the chairs before the audience arrives or given to attenders as they enter the location.

Refreshments   The final consideration of the promotion coordinator is whether to provide refreshments. Refreshments can detract from the show if they are not located in the appropriate place. Refreshments should be located as far from the stage as possible to minimize traffic and noise. They can enhance the show by making the audience more comfortable while viewing the show or afterwards.

Without sales promotion the targeted audience will not be aware of the fashion show. Although personal contact is one of the best methods to attract an audience, it is unrealistic to contact each individual member of the audience. A promotional plan that incorporates various sales promotion methods is the most effective method of reaching the audience. Keeping records of how the audience heard about the show is an effective way to evaluate sales promotion activities and will aid fashion show planners in establishing future sales promotion plans.

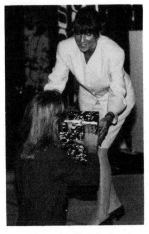

Audience tickets may be used for gift drawings. The anticipation adds an element of excitement to the event.

KEY FASHION SHOW TERMS

advertising	line drawings	radio
advertising units	local advertising	rate card
art	logo	rate costs
body	media list	run-of-paper position rate
clip art	network advertising	sales promotion
copy	paste-up	signage
direct advertising	personal selling	slogan
direct mail advertising	poster	special events
door prizes	press kit	spot advertising
fashion editor	press photograph	subheadline
giveaways	press release	tear sheet
halftones	press show	transit media
headline	publicity	visual merchandising
institutional promotion	public relations	white space
layout	public service announcement	

ADDITIONAL READINGS

1. *Basic Sales Promotion Procedures for Apparel Retailers* (1986). Oklahoma State University, Center for Apparel Marketing.

2. Corinth, *Fashion Showmanship* (1970): The Extras that Make a Good Show Great (Chapter 12).

3. Diehl, *How to Produce a Fashion Show* (1976): Promotional Tie-ins and Giveaways (Chapter 11) and Advertising and Promotion (Chapter 12).

4. Guerin, *Creative Fashion Presentations* (1987): publicizing the market week show (pp 180-189).

5. O'Brien, *Publicity: How to Get It* (1977).

The Merchandise Selection Process

erchandise selection is the designation of apparel, shoes and accessories for presentation in a fashion show to the target customer. Several factors must be considered when selecting merchandise. Most fashion shows are produced to sell clothing. Consequently the merchandise selected for a fashion show must make a clear fashion statement to the audience and be current to the season in order to stimulate sales after the show. The merchandise must be appropriate to the age, sex, income, and lifestyle of the intended audience, and be priced according to what they will spend on fashion. Too many times fashion shows display clothing suitable for the models or show planners, but not the audience. The merchandise must have strong stage appearance to the entire audience regardless of where an individual is seated.

Trade shows will display certain garments out of the current season's line selected to show the depth and breadth of the current line. While the whole line is not presented, the best-selling trends or garments will be repeated many times during the show. These garments may not be selected until hours before the show as the garments are literally finished in the workrooms of the manufacturing facilities just in time for the show.

Consumer shows display merchandise from a specific retailer or group of selected retailers in a geographic area. The fashion show may be sponsored by one store or by a local organization using merchandise from several retailers. Some fashion shows may choose to show merchandise created by artists or designers within the organization or a designer within the community and not found in typical department or specialty stores. These shows are rare, but they are gaining interest. They should be encouraged as the trend for individualized or one-of-a-kind merchandise grows. Consumers are constantly challenging vendors to provide innovative and creative goods. Shows featuring these designers may become a vehicle

The coordination of merchandise and model arrangement must be developed and confirmed in advance of the show (top). Right: Organization of merchandise is crucial to the smooth running of a show. Each model's garments are pulled together.

for artisans/craftspersons to show their creations and can be very successful if produced correctly. Fashion show producers can create the atmosphere of a gallery exhibit with the designer available to the audience following the presentation.

Decisions regarding the **merchandise categories**, which are the divisions of merchandise presented in the show and often correspond to retail departments, are made during the advance planning sessions. Other decisions regarding merchandise categories include clothing classifications and quantities within classifications are also made at this time. Six to eight merchandise categories are regularly used in a fashion show.

Merchandise categories should be divided into two groups. The first category should be clothing that the audience can wear and afford. The second category should be show-stopper items—experimental and/or expensive items—which the audience may not be able to afford but will enjoy viewing and possibly experimenting with after the show. Affordable, wearable clothing should make up 75 percent of the collection with show-stopping garments accounting for 25 percent of the collection. Creating this balance will reassure the audience that the producers know who they are while showing them ways to expand their wardrobe. The industry calls this 75 / 25 percent balance "merchandising to your audience."

The planner for civic or school produced shows should make sure the retail organization selected has enough merchandise of the right types and quantities to match the merchandise categories planned. It is a reflection of poor planning to select a merchandise category and then later realize the retailer carries only limited selections within that category. When retailers agree to lend merchandise for a civic or school show, merchandise categories should be tailored to match the store offerings.

Merchandise should be new to the audience and represent the latest trends to create as much excitement as possible. Merchandise that the audience has already seen in the store will not encourage sales of the goods. Trends may be influenced by past seasons but it is important to select details that reflect the current season. In the commentary explain to the audience how long the trend has been around and the variations which have occurred from season to season.

Using merchandise from more than one retailer has both advantages and disadvantages. The advantages include having more items to choose from and having more categories to draw on for ideas. Small stores which may carry only limited volumes of merchandise also

MERCHANDISE LOAN RECORD

Date _____   Department _____

Store _____

Show _____   Date of Show_____

Issued to _____

Qty	Style #	Size	Color	Description	Price

Received in Stock by _____   Date _____

From _____

Figure 6-1

Merchandise Loan Record

have the opportunity to participate because they do not have to worry about providing large quantities of clothing. It may be considered a disadvantage, using more than one retailer, if favoritism is shown to one store. All retailers should be aware of other participating merchants and the same policies should be enforced for all retailers.

A civic or school group should not try to use a retailer just because they volunteer clothing. Show coordinators may in their excitement use this merchandise only to realize later that the merchandise does not fit the audience. If a junior store, specializing in sizes 3 to 11 aimed at the teenage, young adult market, volunteers merchandise, but the mature audience attending the fashion show purchases missy apparel, sizes 6 to 14, the fashion show will be of little benefit to the merchants or the audience. The merchandise from all the retailers used should match the theme of the show and the needs of the audience.

TIMING

The merchandise selection process should occur after the show theme has been determined. The first step in selecting merchandise for a fashion show by the merchandise selection committee is to visit local retailers to review available merchandise to determine what ideas they can incorporate into the show. This should be planned close enough to the show so that the merchandise selected will be available in retail stores for immediate purchase, but with enough time before the show to avoid last-minute time conflicts. The type of show and the audience will determine how long it will take to select the merchandise.

Merchandise should not be reserved at this time. It may be important to visit a store two or three times to investigate new arrivals especially during seasonal transition periods. The merchandise selection committee needs to be familiar with the fashion preferences of the local market so they can know what merchandise to select.

Ideal Chart

Merchandise is selected to fit the fashion show theme according to a plan called an **ideal chart**. An ideal chart lists all categories of merchandise that will be represented in the show. Within each category the important trends or looks are listed so that they will not be missed when selecting merchandise. The number of garments per category to be pulled will also be listed. These numbers may be double the amount that will actually be used in the show. Important accessories for the season should also be included on the same or separate ideal chart to avoid missing an important trend or idea for the season. These charts should be completed before merchandise is physically pulled from the stores.

RELATIONSHIPS WITH MERCHANTS

When borrowing merchandise from retailers it is important to project a professional image. Merchants may be very reluctant to participate if they feel they have been taken advantage of in the past. A good working relationship with retailers is crucial if the show is to be a

Figure 6-2

Ideal Chart

```
                        IDEAL CHART


     GOOD MORNIN' - Sleepwear - 15 pieces
        t-shirts
        gowns - flannel, satin, long, short
        robes - terry, flannel, satin
        teddies, other lingerie
        gown & robe coordinates
     WORKIN' OVERTIME - Businesswear - 25 pieces
        suits - straight skirt, pleated skirt
        separates - jackets, skirts, trousers
        blouses - seasonal colors
        tailored dresses - double breasted
     GOING THROUGH THE MOTIONS - Workout Wear - 15 pieces
        leotards - earth tones, neon
        tights - footed, capri
        bike pants
        t-shirts
        two piece sets
     YOU CAN LEAVE YOUR HAT ON - Leisurewear - 25 pieces
        sweats - two piece sets, NAU motifs
        sweaters
        jeans
        shorts - jams, tie-dye
     GIRLS JUST WANT TO HAVE FUN - Eveningwear - 20 pieces
        cocktail dresses
        rayon pants
        silk blouses
        little black dresses - strapless
```

success. When approaching merchants to borrow merchandise have as much information about the show as possible to give credibility to the show.

In most cases all the merchandise used in the show is "on loan" from stores. Show personnel are accountable for any lost or damaged merchandise and will be held accountable when the merchandise is returned. Merchandise loan procedures vary from store to store. Ask the merchant how inventory records should be maintained to account for the borrowed merchandise. It is best to ask each store what they prefer.

If no preference is expressed provide a merchandise loan record. A merchandise loan record is a standardized form used to record details of the borrowed merchandise. The loan record should include a description of the garment, manufacturer, color, size, price, date of loan, store authorization, department, where the merchandise is when it is removed from the store, when it will be returned, and who will be responsible for returning the merchandise. A copy should be kept by the store loaning the merchandise and the person responsible for the return of the merchandise. Inform the merchant of the security measures which will be taken to insure the safety of the garments while out of the store.

MERCHANDISE QUANTITY

When planning the merchandise for a show, plan for a minimum of one garment per minute. Designer shows use this minimal number of garments. Many shows plan one ensemble every 30 seconds to hold the audience's attention. A 45-minute show presents a minimum of 45 garments with a maximum of 90 garments, customarily using a quantity between the minimum and maximum number. Most shows do not exceed one hour, 15 minutes for non-fashion portions of the event including refreshments and announcements, and 45 minutes for fashion presentation.

MERCHANDISE PULL

A merchandise pull is the physical removal of merchandise from the sales floor to an area reserved for storage of fashion show merchandise. Twice as many garments should be pulled as will be shown at the beginning of the show preparation to avoid problems during the fittings and presentation of the show. By pulling extra merchandise you will be able to avoid any last-minute frantic searches for replacements if merchandise selected does not fit a model or into the theme of the show, or if it is sold before the show.

Pulling the merchandise should begin two to four weeks before the show date to give ample time for fittings, pressing, and deciding the final lineup of the show merchandise. Basic seasonal items may be pulled first while new looks may not be available until closer to show time. Merchandise for apparel mart shows is often pulled 24 to 48 hours in advance of the show.

GROUPING MERCHANDISE

Merchandise selection also includes grouping or coordinating the merchandise into specific categories to make a series of fashion statements. There should be a rhythm or flow between the groupings. Merchandise within categories must be grouped in a pleasing manner. Pieces within a group may be classified according to color, styling details, sophistication of the designs, popularity of the trend, or some other identifiable theme. The specific categories should have been selected in the planning stage of the fashion show, and confirmed using the ideal chart. After reviewing merchandise available from merchants, groupings of merchandise should be formed. Common categories for merchandise grouping include: *play/casual clothing, career/business clothing, leisure/active/sport clothing, cocktail/evening clothing,* and *bridal/special occasion clothing.* Variations of these categories based on the theme are common in many shows. A show may divide activewear and leisurewear into two categories if enough merchandise is available. Some shows will be based on only one category such as bridalwear or lingerie. A bridal show may classify the merchandise according to styling details such as Victorian dresses, sophisticated dresses, traditional dresses, and attendant accessories. A lingerie show may classify the garments according to fabric type such as silks, jerseys, flannels, and terrycloth.

Figure 6-3

Merchandise

Planning Chart

	NUMBER OF ENSEMBLES	NUMBER OF MODELS	TIME (minutes)
Small Show	25 - 40	4 - 6	20 - 25
Medium Show	40 - 65	8 - 10	25 - 40
Large Show	66 or more	12 or more	40 - 60

When grouping merchandise the audience should always be considered. The first and last categories must make the strongest fashion statements. The first sequence must capture the attention of the audience. The last sequence must leave the audience with a positive attitude toward the fashion show and an urgency to try on the fashions viewed.

The merchandise flow must allow for the audience to see how garments not shown together may be worn together. Do not throw pieces together in any order and expect the audience to know what separate pieces might be worn together as they are shopping after the show. Several mix and match pieces should be shown in succession rather than at the beginning and end of the category.

Models may switch garments, such as jackets, on the runway to show the audience how they might mix and match the pieces shown. It may also be possible to show the audience how to mix pieces they already own with the new pieces of the show.

Usually fashion shows start with the most casual merchandise and build to the most dramatic. Excitement should build throughout the show.

MERCHANDISE LINEUP

When the grouping of the merchandise is completed, it is necessary to create a show lineup. The lineup, a term borrowed from competitive sports, refers to an organized listing of models, the order in which they will appear, and the outfit they will be wearing. A tentative lineup is prepared that includes the order of the models and the merchandise from the groupings (without input from fittings). The lineup is created using the model order—the rotation order in which the models will appear throughout the show. The merchandise is in tentative order. If the lineup has to be changed the coordinator must try to change the order of the merchandise without upsetting the grouping established. Changing the order of the models should be a last resort for this adds confusion during the presentation. Changes in the lineup are made during the fitting and rehearsal sessions. These changes result in a final lineup—a complete listing of merchandise and models in order of their appearance—which is prepared and distributed to everyone after the dress rehearsal.

The final lineup is used for many different purposes throughout the show. Dressing areas are organized according to this lineup, placing models in specific areas to avoid confusion. The dressers, fitters, backstage manager, and cue personnel have an order to follow. Choreographers, music and lighting technicians can record any cues on their copies of the lineup. Commentary can be written and organized using the final lineup.

TENTATIVE LINEUP	
Order of Appearance	Model
SLEEPWEAR SEGMENT	
1	Angel
2	Michelle
3	Becky
4	Stephanie
5	Kathleen
6	Cindy
7	Rachel
8	Tina
9	Mary Kay
10	Kristin
11	Jennifer
12	Pam
13	Kari
14	Lisa
15	Angel
16	Michelle
17	Becky
18	Stephanie
19	Kathleen
BUSINESS SEGMENT	
20	Cindy
21	Rachel
22	Tina
23	Mary Kay
24	Kristin
25	Jennifer
26	Pam
27	Kari
28	Lisa

FINAL LINEUP			
Order of Appearance	Model	Outfit	Props
GOOD MORNIN'			
1	Angel	Mickey nightshirt	teddy
2	Michelle	pink nightshirt	teddy
3	Becky	green nightshirt	teddy
4	Stephanie	royal gown/robe	—
5	Kathleen	cranberry nightshirt	—
6	Cindy	red crop t/boxers	alarm
7	Rachel	green crop t/boxers	—
8	Tina	eyelet gown	rose
9	Mary Kay	navy short gown	—
10	Kristin	navy pajamas	—
11	Jennifer	navy long gown	—
12	Pam	navy robe	—
13	Kari	peach pajamas	TV remote
14	Lisa	mint terry robe	—
15	Angel	yellow terry robe	—
16	Michelle	white gown/robe	—
17	Becky	pink gown/robe	—
18	Stephanie	blue gown/robe	—
19	Kathleen	yellow gown/robe	—
WORKIN' OVERTIME			
20	Cindy	navy coatdress	newspaper
21	Rachel	black suit	briefcase
22	Tina	red suit	briefcase
23	Mary Kay	gray suit	glasses
24	Kristin	navy trenchcoat	—
25	Jennifer	khaki trenchcoat	—
26	Pam	red trenchcoat	—
27	Kari	purple knit dress	—
28	Lisa	turquoise knit dress	—

Figure 6-4 (left) and 6-5 (right) Compare the information on the tentative lineup and the information listed on the final lineup .

MERCHANDISE FITTINGS

Fittings are planned and executed when the tentative lineup is completed. Fittings involve matching the models to the merchandise. It is important to organize fitting sessions to avoid wasted time on the part of models, coordinators, and merchants. If professional models are being used, they are reimbursed for their time at fittings and this cost must be budgeted. Shows involving only a few models may have individual fittings. Shows involving 15 or 20 models should schedule three or four models at a time to avoid mass confusion within the store. Apparel mart or trade shows may use a standard fitting model. When professional models are used to wear clothing in the show, the fitting may be the first time they wear the garments.

Some retailers will reserve a specific area in which show coordinators and models can work. Other retailers with limited space may ask show staff to work around customers and dressing rooms. With retailers it is critical to act professionally and not distract the store's clients.

Fitting Supplies

Before the fittings it is necessary to gather materials that may be needed. A fitting room checklist should be used to avoid forgetting important items. Once a fitting room checklist has been designed, it may be used repeatedly for many shows. Fitting room checklists should include the following items: fitting sheets, model cards, garment tags, pens, pencils, and staplers for recordkeeping. Straight pins, safety pins, tailor's chalk, scissors, and measuring tapes should be available to assist with alterations. Miscellaneous materials to help protect the merchandise including cellophane tape, masking tape for protecting shoes, garment bags to keep accessories together, hangers, dress shields, scarves to protect garments from model's makeup should also be part of fitting supplies. Accessories and foundation garments should also be gathered.

Pre-Fitting Organization

Model sizes must be known, and the merchandise tentatively selected, ordered, and matched to the model before he or she arrives for the fittings. In ideal situations a model should arrive at a prearranged time and find specific ensembles waiting. The ensembles are fitted to the model, alterations or corrections are made, and he or she is able to leave in a timely manner. Store staff should be included when fitting merchandise to models. The retailers know the limitations of alterations and how the merchandise should look. Ask merchants if store seamstresses are available or offer to provide a qualified alterations specialist to make the necessary adjustments to the garments. Costs for alterations should be known in advance and included on the budget, if necessary. These costs should also include any changes made to restore garments to their original state after the show.

Accessories should be bagged and positioned near the merchandise they will be worn with to allow models and dressers smooth changes. (*WWD*)

In the worst case scenario—all the models arrive at the same time to find that the merchandise has not been selected or pulled and their sizes were not known by the show producers. Merchants are disappointed at the lack of professionalism and leadership within the group. Precious time is wasted, tempers flare, and the attitudes of all involved become very negative at a crucial time in the show preparation.

To avoid this scenario plan fittings ten days to two weeks before the show and be fully prepared. The coordinator for school or civic groups should not show a lack of organization to the retailer or the models. Use the tentative lineup and know the specific merchandise that each model will wear before they arrive for the fitting. Do not allow personal preferences of the models to interfere with the merchandise order. Garments should only be exchanged among models if size or fit problems occur. If a garment cannot be fit to a specific model, it may be necessary to discard the garment from the lineup and use a substitute rather than find a model who may fit the garment but upset the flow of merchandise. It may be advisable to have each model fit into several extra garments at the fittings so later substitutions may be made within the lineup without calling the model for a second fitting.

Fitting Sheets

A fitting sheet should be prepared for each outfit as the tentative lineup is determined. The fitting sheet is an information sheet coordinated to the merchandise. It should include sizing information, the order number in the lineup, and a very detailed description of the garment.

Figure 6-6
Fitting Sheet

Making sure the model and the merchandise are complementary takes place at the fittings. The lineup sheet can be finalized after the models try on garments. (*WWD*)

The description must be so detailed that anyone could locate the item within the store by reading it. During the fittings coordinators and models should list accessories, shoes, and hosiery to be worn with the ensemble during the show. If an accessory must be worn in a certain way this information must be included. The coordinator may choose to put the models name on the fitting sheet prior to the fittings if the model order will not be altered. If the garment is of such importance that it has to be included regardless of who wears it then the model's name should be added when it is determined who will wear it. Fitting sheets and copies are used to prepare the final lineup. One set of fitting sheets should be organized in notebook form to serve as a running checklist as accessories are gathered and alterations are completed. At the conclusion of the fittings, commentary will be written using the fitting sheets.

Garment Tags

As fitting sheets are completed each outfit should be labeled with a garment tag which will remain on the merchandise as it is readied for the show. The garment tags should contain

When preparing the merchandise backstage, tags should be removed or hidden. Some garments may require pressing or steaming.

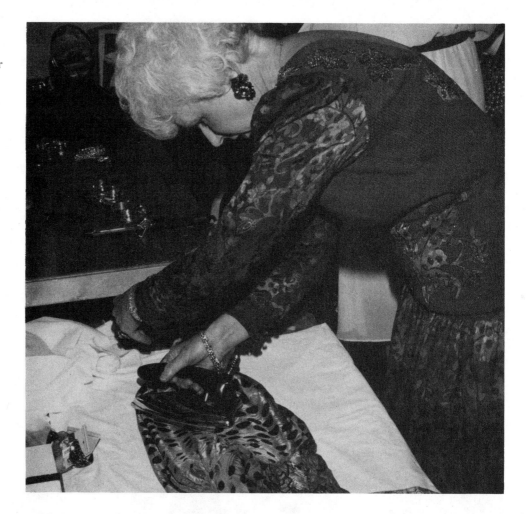

the model's name, brief description of the garment, and the category number. Garment tags will identify merchandise, which has been sent out to be altered or pressed, when it is returned and placed in its appropriate position in the lineup.

Model Cards

Model cards may be used as an alternative to fitting sheets. Fitting sheets are organized by outfit. Model cards are information cards coordinated to the model instead of the merchandise. Information should include the model's name, height, and shoe, hosiery and foundation sizes. Model cards are used in conjunction with commentary cards. A commentary card is filled out for each garment at the time of fittings and exact merchandise details can be noted which may not be obvious when the garment is displayed on a hanger. Both fitting sheets and model cards are not necessary. It should be decided when the models are selected which cataloging system will be used for the show. Fitting sheets allow for easiest organization of the lineup before the show, while model cards allow for the easiest organization of the dressing area during the show. Regardless of which system is used the following information should be obtained for each model: name, address, phone, dress, blouse, suit, skirt, pant, shoe, and head size. Eye and hair coloring should be noted. Male models should list shirt, suit, sport coat, pant, and shoe sizes.

MERCHANDISE PREPARATION

After the fittings, merchandise is prepared for the **dress rehearsal**, a walk-through with garment changes of the show. The dress rehearsal most often involves packing and transferring merchandise and accessories to the show location. Shoes must be packed in their original boxes to keep them clean as they may be sold as merchandise after the show. Heels and soles of shoes that will be sold as merchandise after the fashion show should be taped. Masking tape or heavy duty tape, not transparent or cellophane tape, should cover the entire sole of the shoe and heel to prevent scratches from the floor as the model walks across the dressing area, stage, and runway. Leather goods must be wrapped to avoid scarring. Hats should not be crushed. Clothing should be covered with garment or plastic bags to avoid being soiled in transit.

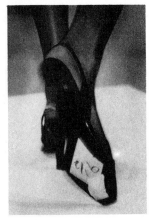

The bottom of shoes should be taped to avoid being scratched and marred as they are worn by the models during the show. *(WWD)*

Once the merchandise has been transported to the show location it must be prepared for the show. All garments should be pressed or steamed to eliminate wrinkles. This will have to be done again after the dress rehearsal and before the performance. With the store's approval all hangtags should be removed. These tags should be kept in a secure location so they may be replaced after the show. If merchants do not want tags removed they should be pinned or taped carefully into the garment so they are not visible to the audience. Merchandise should be returned to the retailers in the same condition it was received— clean, neat, tagged, and ready for sale.

Merchandise selection is a very involved process. Goods must be identified to attract the specific target market of the fashion show. Considerations of demographic information and lifestyle orientations of the consumer must be reviewed in merchandise selection to ensure sales. Also these products must make a strong visual impact and a strong fashion statement. Many people are involved—individuals within the fashion show team and retailers providing the merchandise. The responsibility of selecting merchandise should not be taken lightly. Only a very professional individual who understands the vastness of the task assigned should be considered as coordinator.

KEY FASHION SHOW TERMS

dress rehearsal	ideal sheet	merchandise selection
final lineup	lineup	model card
fitting	merchandise categories	model order
fitting sheet	merchandise loan record	tentative lineup
garment tag	merchandise pull	

ADDITIONAL READINGS

1. Corinth, *Fashion Showmanship* (1970): Be Kind to the Merchandise (Chapter 9).

2. Diehl, *How to Produce a Fashion Show* (1976): Planning the Merchandise: Garments and Accessories (Chapter 5).

3. Goschie, *Fashion Direction and Coordination:* The Fashion Show: Models and Merchandise (Chapter 7).

7

Selecting and Training Models

Models are the individuals engaged to wear the apparel and accessories for a fashion show. They must be able to effectively promote the image of the clothing to the audience in a believable manner, and are very important to the image and success of the fashion show. Models may also infer a standard of excellence, something to be copied. Many people are inspired on how to wear and accessorize their clothing by watching and imitating fashion models.

Models should be attractive, not necessarily "beautiful." The audience should be able to enjoy the model's appearance, but the model's looks should not deter from the merchandise being presented. A flair for fashion as well as an instinct about how clothing and accessories should be worn is helpful. Models are often asked to exercise their fashion sense in showing clothing to its best.

The model should be well groomed and immaculate. Good hair and skin are necessary qualities. The model's figure should be well proportioned and as close to sample sizes as possible. Alterations are expensive and time-consuming. Most standard sample sizes are misses 6 or 8. The minimum height for a standard model is 5' 7".

Whether you are using an amateur or professional model, all models should project a professional attitude. A professional attitude involves being cooperative with the fashion show staff and other models. Moodiness and self-indulgence have no place behind the hectic scene of the fashion show.

The backstage pace is chaotic. When the model rushes to change clothes, she jumps out of one outfit and quickly puts on another with the dresser's assistance. Despite the tension of getting out of and into outfits, the model must be able to promptly gain composure before walking out on the runway. The model must also be able to keep her poise when mistakes or unexpected events happen. A prop might be forgotten, a zipper might break or a shoe strap slips off—the model must be able to gracefully cover up such problems.

Demanding schedules prevail during market weeks, a model may do as many as four or five strenuous shows in one day. The model must maintain a fresh, enthusiastic, and energetic attitude throughout each show. With experience professional models develop an intuition to sense what to do in any circumstance.

Models do not have to personally like the particular garments they are wearing. They should respect the clothes and be able to communicate the appreciation of the look or theme of the garments to the audience.

TYPES OF MODELS

The type of show being produced, the targeted audience, and the merchandise selected, will determine the category or type of model to be featured in the show. The models selected may fit into various categories such as junior, mature, or sophisticated high fashion.

Models fit into various specialty markets in today's fashion industry. Fashion show production may require a variety of different specialties or emphasize just one type. This depends upon the type of show and audience. Specialty groups include male, children, junior, missy, petite, plus size, senior, and high fashion.

Since the 1960s, when interest in men's fashion received a boost, male models have become important to the production of fashion shows for the male trade market as well as in

At the Galeries Lafayette show, male and female models wear clothing from various departments.

consumer shows. Male models can offer a strong appeal to a consumer-oriented show featuring women's and men's wear.

Child models are most often needed to display merchandise for toddler, children, boys, girls, and preteen markets. Additionally they are also featured for the back-to-school season. Professional child models can start training between the ages of five and ten.

Children are great audience pleasers during shows, but caution must be used to avoid unpleasant scenes. It is very difficult to work with children under the age of five. Young children may appear able to handle modeling during rehearsals, but become frightened when placed on a runway with a large number of strangers staring at them. Small children have cried or acted in poor taste when frightened on stage.

If the show planners decide to use children, the following suggestions may help to avoid unpleasant situations. First, try to identify children who act somewhat mature even if they do not understand the idea of a fashion show. These children should know that strangers may have to dress or otherwise handle them. It may be helpful to have the children practice in front of an audience made up of show staff and others to make them feel more at ease in front of a crowd. Mothers or adults supervising the children should understand the responsibilities of models. The adult must be willing to watch over the child during all rehearsals of the show but not interfere with the show.

Junior models are between the ages of 13 and 17. Depending how old the model looks and what size he or she wears, this model can cover the back-to-school market. Girls and boys younger than 13 would wear sizes 4 to 6x, and they would wear larger children's sizes as they get older. More extensive fashion shows introducing a new season may have junior models of various ages.

Missy models are generally between the ages of 17 to 22 years of age. Although the model does not have to be in this particular age, these women are between 5'7" and 5'10½". Models in this group have slim figures, wearing standard sample sizes, 6 and 8.

Petite models have increased in popularity with the rapidly expanding petite apparel market. Petite models are approximately 5'2". Most work for petite models is for specialty fashion shows featuring petite merchandise or as manufacturer's fit models. Fit models work in a manufacturer's design area. Sample garments are fit to a standard fit model.

Another category gaining popularity is the plus size model. Recognizing this growth market the fashion industry has hired full figure models to meet the manufacturer and consumer needs. The physical characteristics for this model are: height, 5'7"; bust, 44½"; waist, 36"; and hips, 47". Models for large sizes are used as manufacturers fit models or for fashion shows featuring large size merchandise.

A modeling career was usually over for a woman after she turned 30. With the changing demographics and the population getting older, consumers are readily accepting older role models, and a new category of senior model has emerged. Female models can continue to work for years. The senior model may be gray- or white-haired, at least 40, with a youthful appearance. Some of the high fashion models of the 1950s have found a newly revived modeling career in the 1990s.

High fashion models include a limited number of highly paid women who are internationally known and work for the top international and domestic designers. High fashion

Manufacturers such as Givenchy have created products for specialty markets. This plus size model (left) wears a garment from his special size line. There are a limited number of women in the world who are high fashion models (right). These well-paid models work in Paris, Milan, and New York for the top designers.

models are typically 18 to 35 years old. Height is a minimum of 5'8", but may range to 6 feet tall. They travel from one country to the next, where their services as sophisticated image makers are needed. High fashion models work in the international fashion world as runway models. They are also known for their photographic work, often under exclusive contract to a particular designer or cosmetics firm.

RESOURCES FOR MODELS

Professional models are trained in modeling techniques and are hired through modeling agencies or schools. Amateur models are not trained as professional models and are selected from other resources. Some effective resources for obtaining models include: a retail store's fashion advisory board, the store's customers and personnel, the membership of the organization sponsoring the event, or performing arts schools.

Modeling agencies are companies that represent a variety of fashion models and act as scheduling agents for the models. When the decision is made to use professional models, the show planners should contact the agency and ask to see any models that they might consider for the show. Headsheets or model books provided by the agency will enable the show model committee to evaluate the look and experience of the professional models prior to an initial visit called a "go see." Image as well as runway show experience should be considered when hiring professional models.

Models bring their portfolios to the "go see." Their portfolio contains examples of photographic work and fashion show experience in addition to test shots. There is no fee for this initial visit. The show planners may ask the model to try on a garment to help in the evaluation of her appearance and image. If the look is appropriate for the show being produced, the model is "booked." Quickly booking the model for the show date through his or her agency is essential. The best models are generally booked well in advance and may be unavailable. The person in charge of models should confirm in writing the selection of models, date, time, and rate with the booker at the model agency.

Modeling schools, specializing in training men, women and children in modeling techniques, are another resource for models. These schools exist in every major city. Classes may involve such activities as runway methods, makeup application for photography or runway, hairstyling, voice, figure control, and new modeling procedures. Many modeling schools provide agency services, booking students or models after they finish their training for jobs.

Amateur models generally have a personal interest in fashion and are willing to participate in fashion shows without any reimbursement. Amateur models are trained by show personnel. One type of amateur model may be a participant on a store's fashion advisory board. These advisory panels are organized by retailers to obtain consumer information about the store. Board members may be asked to serve as advisors regarding merchandise and services, salespersons or models for fashion shows. Stores may have various advisory panels for different specialty markets such as teens, college or career women. Another source of amateur models is the store's customers and employees. Regular and loyal patrons of a particular store may have the fashion image and status within the community to partici-

Amateur models can come from many sources including schools and civic organizations. They have great enthusiasm to compensate for limited training.

pate in the store's promotion. Employees of the company also project the store's image. Customers may be offered a discount on purchases as compensation for their participation. Store employees may be paid regular wages during the fittings, rehearsals, and show presentation.

The organization sponsoring the fashion show for a benefit may have members who are interested in modeling. Groups such as the Junior League, or auxiliaries for the local symphony or performing arts company may provide models for charity shows. Socially prominent local women can add local interest and prestige to an event. Group members may have had some model training or fashion experience to help with modeling.

Students in fashion or performing arts schools are often eager participants in fashion shows. They will often participate in fashion shows just for the fun and experience of being involved. Actors and dancers have often enjoyed taking part in fashion shows. The theatrical aspects of the fashion show have benefitted from participation by people trained in theatrical techniques. Many fashion shows feature dancing numbers and choreography, using dancers to their best advantage. Trained dancers are often willing to teach dance steps to models without prior dance education.

PROFESSIONAL VERSUS AMATEUR MODELS

The decision to use professional versus amateur models is frequently dependent upon the show budget. Professional models must be paid. Shows working with a limited budget may be restricted to using amateur models and offering a gift, discount or gift certificate to the model in lieu of payment. This helps to ensure a positive feeling among all the parties involved. It may also encourage purchases at the store. Many fashion show directors feel that despite the cost of using professional models, they create a smoother, more masterful show. Experienced models can handle last-minute changes and the confusion associated with fashion show production. They have developed an authoritative attitude in presenting clothes properly. This confidence shows as the professional model walks down the runway. Trained models are quick to pick up modeling patterns and routines. Directions and cues are easily learned and remembered. Appointments are responsibly met. Clothing and accessories are taken care of and respected. Any unforseen problems or emergencies are maneuvered with expert execution.

Professional models are often able to make excellent suggestions about how to wear or accessorize an outfit based on their years of experience and love for the clothing. Pros know how to stress the importance of the clothes rather than themselves.

The success or failure of months of fashion show preparation can depend upon the performance of the models. Many amateur models take their role very seriously. Unfortunately some of the disaster stories regarding fashion shows come from the ranks of unprepared amateur models. Without some training and direction, amateur models have flown down runways with arms flapping like birds, others have frozen with fear on the runway after seeing the audience. Untrained models have destroyed clothes by not taking proper care of them. Amateur models demand more time and attention due to their lack of experience. The show may require more amateur than professional models since it will take them longer to change garments.

When selecting the amateur model, the model committee needs to be sure that the model is willing to make a commitment to participate in fittings, rehearsals, and the show. Being a model is not the glamorous job many amateurs think it is.

If members of a civic club are selected to model, the model committee must use diplomacy in selecting and training participants. Since these members are not always standard model sizes and often have very strong opinions about what they want to wear, the model committee and merchandise committee must be ready to handle objections with tact. Inexperienced models may not understand that a fashion show is an important part of doing business for the store or manufacturer providing the clothes. They may resist wearing anything they dislike.

Amateur models have a great drawing power. Audiences love to see their friends and relatives participating in fashion shows. It can certainly add to the audience's enjoyment of the show. Another reason amateur models contribute to a show is the believability factor. When friends and relatives see garments on "real people," they can see themselves wearing the clothes. Professional models often look so sophisticated, customers cannot see themselves in the garments.

Any union rules that may affect the show and the models should be investigated. Shows that are held in television studios, convention halls, or theaters might be influenced by union activities. The specifications may bias the selection of models and their compensation.

Photographic versus Runway Models Top name designers such as Ralph Lauren, Bill Blass or Calvin Klein may insist upon using photographic models for their runway shows. Photographic models require higher fees than models who do straight runway

Ethnic minority models are quite popular.

modeling. Although there has been a blurring of these two separate careers, some models continue to specialize.

TRAINING MODELS

Walking, timing, posing, and turning are very important aspects of the model's presentation on the runway. Confidence and ease in executing these attributes are instrumental for the professional appearance of the fashion show. Professional models are well-trained and have experience. The show's model crew or choreographer will need to work with the amateur models.

The model must walk with a smooth light pace. Body weight should be forward. The body should be straight, but not stiff. Arms are placed down at the side seams of the garment with palms toward the body. They should be kept loose and easy and not swing out from the body. Hands and arms may be used to feature some design element such as a pocket of the costume. Using hands gracefully is important to modeling. Hands should be relaxed. A slight bend to the wrist is more attractive than a perfectly rigid, straight arm. Placing the hand in a ballet position or bend will be more becoming. Shoulders should be down, back and relaxed. The stomach should be flat and buttocks tucked under. The steps should be just long enough to keep the body erect. Reach with the front foot and push with the back foot for the appearance of walking on air. Feet should follow an imaginary straight line on the floor.

Models and the commentator are responsible for the timing of the show. The speed and pace of walking or dancing can accelerate or prolong the show. Models can remain on the runway for longer periods of time, giving other models time to change or get ready, by repeating the basic pattern of walking and turns.

Amateur models frequently walk too fast or want to get off the runway quickly. One technique that helps to keep the pace at a good level is to stop and pose on the runway. If a photographer is used, the models could be trained to pose at the end of the runway and wait for a photograph to be taken. This cue will help to slow down the pace of a fast-moving model.

Runway turns are known as pivots. Smooth, graceful and continuous motion are ideal for runway turns. The half turn is essential for this movement and accomplished by turning on the balls of the feet. No weight is placed on the heels. Put one foot in front of the other. If the right foot is forward turn to the left. If the left foot is forward turn right. With both knees flexed turn to the opposite direction (180 degrees) smoothly. The body turns halfway, front to back and from the back to the front to reverse directions. Models should practice this until it is performed flawlessly.

The walking pivot combines a number of steps with the half turn. Take three steps. On the fourth step, make it a short one. Make a half turn and turn around. This combination can be used at any point on the runway as directed by the choreographer.

Sometimes models are asked to make turns simultaneously with other models. Practicing and perfecting turns with other models makes this look very effective.

Expression and personality are often overlooked in the technical aspects of walking, turning, and posing. Smiling is a positive expression to show that the model likes what she is wearing. The model must be able to communicate a variety of emotions depending upon

Figure 7-1

Individual Model Lineup

Sheet

| | Name of Model_____ |
| | Name of Show_____ |

Order of Appearance	Description of Apparel	Hosiery	Shoes	Accessories Props

The Individual Model Lineup Sheet lists merchandise ensembles in order of appearance.

NAME OF MODEL: JOY

NAME OF SHOW: NIPON / DILLARDS

#	DESCRIPTION OF OUTFIT	LEGWEAR/SHOES	JEWELRY	ACCESSORIES PROPS	NEEDS
7	LODEN JERSEY JUMPSUIT	BLK OPAQUE / BLK. SUEDE	-ear	BLK. JERSEY GLOVES	TRIPLE W/ TANY + TINA [center]
20	TRI-TONE WOOL CREPE SUIT	BLK. OPAQUE / BLK. LEATHER		BLK LEATHER GLOVE	DBL W/ TANYA
34	GREY FLANNEL COATDRESS GOLD BRAID	NUDE GOLD SANDAL	-ear	X	TRIPLE W/ TANYA + KIMBERLY
47	BLK CREPE SUIT LAMÉ DRAPED COLLAR	NUDE GOLD SANDAL	ear	X	DOUBLE W/ KIMBERLY
60	GOLD LACE TOP / GOLD GAZAR SKT.	NUDE GOLD SANDAL	+ bangle	X	DOUBLE W/ BELJANA

the type of merchandise or show. The model may be called upon to act in any manner from casual to elegant. If the outfit is fun or casual a smile is very appropriate. On the other hand if the item being presented is sophisticated or serious a smile may seem out of place. It is important for the model to practice various expressions in a mirror.

Stage entrances vary. Sometimes there will be an archway or a screen to walk through, or possibly a platform to step on. The show choreographer will direct the models regarding entrances. It may be necessary to pose near a screen or simply walk down the runway. The show choreographer will provide direction for exits. One graceful method is to do a simple half turn and face the audience. After a brief pose another half turn will position the model to walk off the stage.

NUMBER AND ROTATION OF MODELS

There are no hard and fast rules determining the number of models needed for a show. The show organizers need to know how many models will be in a show, and how long each model will need to change between outfits. Adequate time must be arranged for models to change outfits.

Setting up a rotation schedule for models will help the show run smoothly. One way to use models effectively is to arrange a specific order for the models for the first scene prior to the fittings. Then keep the models in approximately the same order throughout the show. For example if 15 models are needed for a show these 15 models are placed in order. In this way model #1 would always be before model #2 and after #15. The audience will not be able to detect that models are always in the same order, but the plan gives models adequate time to change. It also helps models to recognize the order established.

Each model should be made fully aware of the outfits that he or she will be wearing and the order the garments should be worn. The **Individual Model Lineup Sheet** helps to clarify the model's order of appearance, outfit, shoes, hosiery, accessories, props, and whether the model is alone or part of a group.

Depending upon the number of outfits, type of show, facilities, and experience of the models, a 30 to 40 minute show may use as few as five or as many as 20 models. A market show in New York generally lasts about 30 minutes. During that time 75 to 100 garments are presented. With that large number of garments to show and to make a visual statement two or three models and sometimes as many as ten models are on the runway at one time. The number of models will increase as the distance between the dressing and stage areas increases. Four or more extra models may be necessary if the dressing area is not on the same floor as the stage area.

A rough guideline for the number of models can be based upon the size of the show being presented.

Size of Show	Number of Models
Small	4 to 6
Medium	8 to 10
Large	12 or more

Figure 7-2
Model List

MODEL LIST

Name of Show_____Date_____

Name	Phone Number	Size	
		Garment	Shoe
Angel Thomas	523-7127	6	8 1/2N
Michelle Gibson	526-1287	8	9N
Becky Points	774-3226	8	8M
Stephanie Hiers	779-1718	7	9M
Kathleen Warren	523-1563	6	9N
Cindy Mercier	779-1828	6	8 1/2M
Rachel Anderson	774-5226	6	7 1/2N
Tina Harwood	523-2156	8	8N
Mary Kay Kelly	523-3127	7	8 1/2M
Kristin Mobery	526-1028	6	8N
Jennifer Sherman	525-3134	8	9M
Pam Witte	523-5251	7	8 1/2N
Kari Smith	774-2445	6	8M
Lisa Webster	779-1789	8	9N

Figure 7-3
Female Model Card

FEMALE MODEL CARD

Name _____ Phone No. _____
Address _____
Agency _____ Phone No. _____
Age _____ Category _____
Eye Color _____ Hair Color _____
Dress Size _____ Shoe Size _____
Height _____ Bust _____
Waist _____ Hips _____
Hat Size _____ Glove Size _____

Figure 7-4
Male Model Card

MALE MODEL CARD

Name _____ Phone No. _____
Address _____
Agency _____ Phone No. _____
Age _____ Category _____
Eye Color _____ Hair Color _____
Neck Size _____ Sleeve Length _____
Height _____ Waist _____
Suit size _____ Inseam _____
Hat Size _____ Glove Size _____
Shoe Size _____ Sock Size _____

Models learn makeup techniques from each other and cosmetic specialists backstage. (*WWD*)

When selecting and booking models, the planning staff should have one or two alternative models present to prevent the inevitable disappointment and scramble if it is necessary to replace an absent model. Professional models rarely miss a booking unless there are some extenuating circumstances. However, working with amateur models almost always results in a "no show." Such contingency plans will help to relieve pressures.

Model List

After models have been selected, the model committee should prepare a formal model list. A model list will include the model's name, telephone number, garment, and shoe size. People in charge of working with the models will find this information beneficial.

Model Cards   As discussed in Chapter 6, the model card provides specific characteristics about each model. Separate cards for male and female models are beneficial. These cards have very detailed information about the physical characteristics of the individual models. This information will help the people in charge of the selection of merchandise.

RESPONSIBILITIES OF MODELS

Models have a variety of responsibilities during the fittings, rehearsals, and show production. It is most important that at all times the models associated with a show cooperate with the show personnel. A positive attitude and professionalism are also appreciated by the fitting, rehearsal, production, and clean-up crews.

Responsibilities during Fittings

Fittings are generally scheduled at predetermined intervals, and the models need to be on time. If a model is late, it can throw off the whole schedule. The merchandise selection committee should have a series of garments ready for her when she arrives for fittings. The model should be ready to get right to work trying on clothing. The model should come to the fitting with makeup and hair appropriately fixed and neatly dressed, including wearing pantyhose.

Cooperation by the show staff as well as the models is very important. The model should never mention if she likes a garment, unless asked. That is not an important factor when most items are selected to make a fashion trend or color statement.

Responsibilities during Rehearsals

The rehearsal requires teamwork by all involved. Models should come prepared with a bag containing a few supplies: a complete set of makeup, a selection of accessories such as jewelry, gloves, belts, and scarves, and lingerie such as a strapless brassiere or half slip to use if necessary. An extra pair of sandalfoot pantyhose might be necessary for sandals as well as if hose snags and runs. It can destroy the image of the ensemble when hosiery is not perfect. A seasonal basic shoe wardrobe will help the show coordinators see how a complete ensemble will look. Other items to have include: a scarf, or hood covering, to help protect clothing from makeup as it is tried on, pins, a first aid kit, and clear nail polish. Personal hygiene is very important. Dress shields or extra deodorant might be necessary.

Caring for clothing is a joint responsibility of the show personnel and the model. The model should never pull a garment overhead without a scarf or zip-hood covering, worn to protect clothes from makeup. Merchandise tags should not be removed unless specifically told to do so. Shoes should be removed while stepping into or out of a garment. To protect clothing the model should never sit, eat, drink or smoke while dressed in the garment for the

Organized chaos is often a better term for backstage. *(WWD)*

show. Clothing should be returned to hangers and a proper storage place as soon as possible after trying on and approval.

The model should be neat, clean and pick up personal belongings. The model should not expect the dresser or fitter to be a personal maid. Children and friends should be left at home during fittings and rehearsals. Although children may love to see the process, they would be in the way. Friends may offer helpful suggestions, but they too are in the way.

Responsibilities on the Show Day

Models should be on time and arrive at least thirty minutes before the start of the show, unless given other instructions. This will be enough time to get ready for the show. Models may need the assistance of hair and makeup personnel on the show day. In any case models should arrive with their tote bags with personal supplies as discussed previously.

Although a dresser is assigned to assist the model, the model should check the clothing and accessories to make sure they are arranged in the order that they will be worn for the show. The dresser should prepare the garments by hiding the tags or removing them and putting them in a safe place so that they can be re-attached later when garments are returned to the store. The garments should be ready to step into—zippers are unzipped, buttons unbuttoned, scarves pre-tied if possible. Shoes and jewelry should be lined up. The model should be aware of the model lineup and where the lineup sheets are posted. This protocol should be followed during all rehearsals using clothing and accessories as well as during the show.

Models should step into and out of clothes only while standing on a covered area of the dressing room. Once the model is dressed, he or she must follow the rule not to sit down. In addition the no smoking rule must be adhered to. Food and beverages have no place near the merchandise. The merchandise must be kept in an immaculate condition. It must be able to go back into stock for sale.

Models and dressers should keep conversation to a minimum immediately before and during the show. If it is necessary to speak, use a soft voice. Do not bring children or friends to the backstage or dressing room areas. Help to keep the backstage area free from excess confusion.

Models need to be cooperative. They should dress quickly and line up promptly. Listening to the commentator or backstage starter and watching for any special cues, will help to make everything look smooth and polished.

Models should be pleasant, discreet, and poised. If the model has an accident or makes a mistake, he or she needs to continue without drawing attention to the situation. Such occurrences as tripping on the steps or stage or dropping a prop or accessory are very common. A professional model will just ignore the circumstances and carry on.

EVALUATING MODELS

Any organization utilizing models on a regular basis should set up evaluation criteria. These criteria should be based upon the characteristics discussed earlier. Models that do not live up to these aspects should be eliminated from further consideration.

Model Expectations

Be on time for fittings, rehearsal, and show.

Be cooperative.

Keep merchandise in perfect condition. Clothing and accessories must be ready for sale after the show.

Never sit in an outfit.

Do not eat, smoke or drink around clothing.

Step in and out of clothing in the area with floor protection.

Use a scarf to protect clothing while pulling clothes over the head.

Keep backstage conversation to a minimum, using a low tone voice or whisper.

Dress and undress quickly.

Line up immediately.

Listen to commentator or cue personnel for instructions.

Do not bring friends or children backstage or in the dressing room before, during or after the show.

The fashion office should create a file or record on models who are used for fashion shows regularly. Information should include the name, address, telephone number and relative statistics for each model employed. Measure of performance should be recorded after each show. Simple comments will help show personnel in selecting models for future shows.

The show personnel can expect the models to be on time for the fittings, rehearsal, and the show, be cooperative, provide personal supplies, take care of the merchandise, and dress quickly. A model can be expected to do her own makeup and hair unless the services of a makeup artist and hair stylist are specifically provided. The job of modeling can be exciting and glamorous, but also grueling. These well-groomed, polished individuals provide the image on which the clothing and accessories are exhibited.

KEY FASHION SHOW TERMS

amateur model	junior model	petite model
child model	male model	photographic model
fashion advisory board	missy model	pivot
fit model	model card	plus size model
go see	modeling agency	professional model
headsheet	modeling schools	runway model
high fashion model	model list	senior model
individual model lineup sheet		

ADDITIONAL READINGS

1. Corinth, *Fashion Showmanship* (1970): All about the Models (Chapter 10).

2. Diehl, *How to Produce a Fashion Show* (1976): Models—Choosing, Training and Evaluating Them (Chapter 7).

3. Goschie, *Fashion Direction and Coordination* (1986): The Fashion Show: Models and Merchandise (Chapter 7).

4. Lenz, *The New Complete Guide of Fashion Modeling* (1982).

8

Commentary

Commentary is the oral delivery of descriptive details of the garments and accessories presented in a fashion show. It is used to entertain the audience and make clear fashion statements to help sell the merchandise. The commentary should complement the clothing not distract the audience from the fashions being shown. Good commentary tells the audience something about the garments that they cannot readily see from viewing the garments. Enjoyable commentary can make the audience and the models feel at ease. An inadequate or poor commentary can harm the relationship between the audience and the organization or retailer.

Audiences today are stimulated more through visual than audio presentations, consequently they do not always require a descriptive or analytical narration. Therefore commentary is an optional element of fashion show production. Particularly in fashion, viewers can learn more from observing details than from hearing about the details. This is especially true in large metropolitan areas where fashion trends appear sooner. Fashions may be seen in store windows, magazines, and on other individuals. People do not have to hear about the fashions. In smaller communities, fashion may be seen in magazines or on television before the actual pieces arrive in the stores. These areas are more likely to use commentary at fashion shows to provide more complete details about the upcoming trends.

Consumer-oriented shows are more likely to use commentary. The commentary may be very informative giving every detail to the customer, pointing out seasonal selling features to convince the audience to purchase the fashions after the show. Many clients attend fashion shows to identify new looks. Sophisticated audiences may be able to identify looks easily but less fashion-aware audiences want reinforcement about their interpretation of future trends. These audience members want information about the fashions. Commentary is used to emphasize important fashion ideas for the season.

The commentator is a member of the show staff with the designated responsibility of preparing and delivering the commentary during the show. He or she is perceived to be a fashion expert and expected to interpret the trends for them.

Initially commentary should tie the theme and the fashions of the show together. The narration allows for easy transition from one segment to the next without confusing the audience. For example a show entitled, "So Many Clothes, So Little Time," shows fashions worn by professional women throughout the day. One segment may show business attire for the office while the next segment may show workout clothing for aerobics. Without commentary explaining that in the 1990s many businesswomen are exercising at local athletic clubs over the lunch hour the audience may not see the correlation of these garments.

In today's busy society it is often necessary to be creative in holding an audience's attention. Commentary can do just that. It can keep an audience interested in the fashion show by creatively analyzing what they are viewing. Brass buttons and embroidered crests have new importance when narrated as part of a current trend as in the following example:

> *For big city streets, there's a new four star military trend—top brass details and accessories set these clothes apart from the troops. Historically, crests distinguished English families from each other. This outfit has true class!*

Commentary can set the mood for the show and create excitement in the audience. The right introduction will have the audience primed for what they will be viewing and have them excited about adapting the fashions into their wardrobes. Commentary throughout the show can maintain the excitement by leading the audience to a climax, tying into the exciting finale of eveningwear or bridalwear.

Production personnel often use commentary to set the pace of the fashion show. A show which is proceeding too fast can be slowed by incorporating additional commentary, pauses, or fashion information. If the audience is drifting, commentary can speed up the show by eliminating unnecessary details and pointing out extreme fashion looks. Lineup personnel and models must have some knowledge of the commentary. The starter must know every signal for an entrance called a cue to send the models out and models must know cues in order to stage the fashion show perfectly.

SHOWS NOT USING COMMENTARY

Certain types of fashion shows, such as trade shows used in the secondary market to show fashions to prospective retail buyers, will not use commentary. Instead they will use contemporary music and narrate only style numbers while the audience takes notes in their buying guides which describe the fashions and note price and minimum orders required. Production shows and informal shows are also less likely to use commentary. Production shows staged as theatrical productions will not use commentary because it interferes with the performance. Details about the garments are printed in a program. If commentary is used in a production show it will be very brief and concise presenting a very strong statement at the beginning of each scene to set the mood. This commentary must be very smooth so the audience does not realize their attention is moving back and forth from commentator to fashions. Charity fashion shows featuring current lines of top designers may not use commentary. The fashions speak for themselves requiring no additional narration from a commentator.

Informal shows seldom use commentary because of the restrictions of the show's location. Commentary used at an informal restaurant show would intrude with the conversation among the customers during their meal. If commentary is used at informal shows it should be very conversational and the commentator should take many cues from the audience as to their enjoyment of the commentary. During tea-room modeling the model becomes a commentator, describing the characteristics of her ensemble as she moves from table to table. The model

Commentary for shows produced by students may be accomplished by a team. Students use a variety of references in preparing commentary.

Pros and Cons of Using
Commentary

Pros

Emphasizes important fashion ideas for the upcoming season

Entertains

Holds the audience' attention

Provides transitions between show segments

Interprets trends for the audience

Reinforces the "new looks" of the season

Sets mood of the show

Sets pace of the show

Ties the theme together with the merchandise

Gives descriptive details of the garments to the audience

Cons

Detracts from the visual presentation of the show

Fashions may speak for themselves requiring no additional narration

Interferes with theatrical performances

Location restrictions

should be prepared to respond to individuals from the audience who are interested in additional information. Models should also respect people who wish to be left alone.

COMMENTARY CARDS

As stated in previous chapters, information about models and merchandise is gathered on fitting sheets which are then used to write commentary. A second approach sometimes used by fashion show producers to prepare commentary is to use model cards and commentary cards. Commentary cards are prepared to read as narration during the show, usually on 5" x 8" index cards. These cards are the easiest to read and keep in order during the presentation. If the order of the models is disrupted after the start of the show, the commentator can effortlessly adjust the cards to match models as they make their entrance. Sheets of paper often rustle and cause noise over the sound system.

Commentary cards should include the model's name, the position in the lineup (number and segment for easy reference at the top of the card), a description of the ensemble and accessories, and special selling features. One garment should be included on each commentary card. Commentary cards are best filled out at the time of the fittings. The commentator can see fitting details important to the seasonal trend that may not be obvious when the garment is on a hanger. Skirt lengths will appear in correct proportion when worn by the intended model. It is important to also include selling features of the garments. For example, a washable silk has recently reached the market; a garment made of this fabric should most definitely be described as machine washable to entice the audience to purchase garments made of this fabric.

Co-commentators review their notes before a show.

TYPES OF COMMENTARY

The commentary may include a total description (full commentary) of the garments, a partial description of the garments, or have no description of the garments allowing the commentator to ad lib the commentary. There are four types of commentary:

1. Full commentary
2. Partial commentary
3. Impromptu commentary
4. Script commentary

Each may be used according to the type of show, the expertise, and the preference of the commentator.

Full Commentary

Full commentary involves writing every word of commentary on cards or in script form prior to the show. With full commentary it is important that the commentator deliver the commentary in a natural manner to avoid demonstrating that it was prepared in its entirety before the show. This type of commentary does not allow for last-minute changes in the lineup. A pre-written script follows strict fashion statements, which may be lost with any last-minute changes in the lineup. The commentator may also not have proper filler commentary available in case of any changes or delays.

Partial Commentary

Some commentators are more comfortable using commentary that is less than complete as they stand at the podium—partial commentary is only a portion of the commentary. The major details of the garments may be listed in outline form or written in partial script with very little detail on a card. The description of the fashions and accessories are stated by the commentator as needed. This may be less time-consuming to prepare prior to the show but is more difficult to use during the actual show.

Impromptu Commentary

Impromptu commentary is commentary created spontaneously during the show using only brief cue cards for assistance. It is not written word for word in script form. This type of commentary may sound misleading as if it requires no preparation, but indeed it does require some advanced readiness. The commentator must accumulate fashion phrases on cards to use as a lead off to the scene or to describe each garment. It is important that the commentator have one and one half the number of phrases for the number of garments being used. This may sound like an extreme, but it is important that the commentator have enough buffer commentary to be flexible in case of last-minute changes in the lineup during the show. The cards also provide the commentator with added confidence in describing fashion trends. Impromptu commentary will also be delivered more naturally putting both the commentator and the audience at ease.

Highly experienced commentators such as retail fashion directors who work with current fashions and fashion terminology on a regular basis may choose not to have any prepared

Examples of a full commentary card (top); a partial commentary card (bottom).

Angel Thomas   Good Mornin'   #1

Rise and shine! Up and at em! We can all relate to having a bit of difficulty finding a "zest for life" first thing in the morning. Whether it's not parting with that favorite teddy bear or revealing our attachment to Mickey Mouse, all we care about is tuning that radio to the perfect song to get us out of bed. This Mickey Mouse nightshirt from Cheap Clothes communicates on its own that it's comfortable and that the model is reluctant to change into other clothes.

Angel Thomas   Good Mornin'   #1

GARMENT DESCRIPTION: Mickey Mouse T-shirt motif, knee length

ACCESSORIES: teddy bear, fuzzy slippers, eye mask, radio on stage

PROVIDED BY: Cheap Clothes

---

commentary written. Instead they may review the garments prior to the show and then speak about the garments as they appear on the stage or runway, eliminating time demands prior to the show. This type of commentary allows for the most changes in the model lineup because the commentator is not influenced by the order when commentating. Often the commentator will have a conversational style when speaking and be very spontaneous about the fashions. Designer shows may use the impromptu approach if the designer serves as the show commentator.

Only the most experienced commentators can do this with the style needed to influence the audience. Problems occur with impromptu commentary when words or fashion phrases are repeated too often. During a show an inexperienced commentator used the word "adorned" so many times that she lost the attention of her audience. It would have greatly enhanced the commentary to have variety in the descriptions.

Script Commentary

Production shows may use a script commentary. Commentary in script form is full commentary written out word for word for the commentator to read and speak like that of a broadcast. Script commentary is used because it allows for all cues to be noted by the commentator. Scripts are written on pages with two columns. The left-hand column denotes scene, music, lighting, and model cues while the right-hand column cites the actual commentary with planned pauses.

Filler Commentary

Problems may sometimes occur during the show. First, the commentator may become nervous in front of an audience, and deliver the commentary much faster than intended. Second, many commentators believe that they will be able to think creatively on their feet and decide to use partial commentary, which is less time-consuming to prepare prior to the show. However, only during the show do they realize that they cannot think of enough different information to relay to the audience. Also, if they have decided to use impromptu commentary, commentators assume that they have prepared enough commentary. Not until show time do they realize how fast they have used the commentary prepared. To avoid these problems and not be caught off guard, prepare far more commentary than will be used or filler commentary, which can be used at any time during the show to fill in unexpected pauses that may occur. Filler commentary may include fashion and beauty tips, credits to hair and makeup technicians, store services and facilities if produced by a retail store, or other facts of interest to the audience. Each category of filler commentary such as fashion tips or credits should be separated into piles before the show so a variety of comments can be easily accessed during the show.

ELEMENTS OF WRITING COMMENTARY

Commentary should be written to establish a fashion feeling or mood of the clothing. The point of commentary is to distinguish the current seasons clothing from the past season to encourage the audience to update their wardrobes.

"SO MANY CLOTHES, SO LITTLE TIME"
Carriage House at Riordan State Park
April 5, 1992

STAGE	Two 4' x 8' x 18' carpeted runways with stairs on each end place at 45 degree angles in the center of the open area. tape player placed on corner of right runway. Lights focused on center of each stage. Commentator podium stage right.
INTRODUCTION	Background music plays softly. Houselights down. Commentator, Debbie, enters.

Show Begins

DEBBIE	Good evening! Sit back and relax as we journey through a typical day of a '90s woman. After all, there are "So Many Clothes, And So Little Time!"

First model enters and picks up tape player. Sound technicians starts music as model adjusts knob of tape player.

DEBBIE	Rise and Shine! Up and at em! We can all relate to having a bit of difficulty finding a "zest for life" first thing in the morning. Whether it's not parting with that favorite teddy bear or revealing our attachment to Mickey Mouse, all we care about is tuning that radio to the perfect song to get us out of bed. This Mickey Mouse nightshirt from Cheap Clothes communicates on its own that it is comfortable and the model is reluctant to change into other clothes

It should start out incorporating the lifestyle of the audience so they may be aware of how to use the clothing and work towards specifics as the clothing is shown. Fashion shows and commentary fail when the audience presumes the garments are not necessary or appropriate for their lifestyles. Wording should inform the audience of what the garment can do for them as well as what it looks like.

Commentary should describe the clothing to the audience using the most current fashion terminology. Listings of fashion terms or fashion dictionaries should be used to develop the

This season don't get caught off guard asking for a gray, green, purple, or blue blazer at your local retailer. Instead show your fashion knowledge by asking for charcoal, spruce, plum or cadet blue. Let the fashion consultant be impressed by your up-to-date knowledge of fashion colors for the season.

correct statement for each ensemble. The correct names of sleeves, closures, decorative details, and other construction components should be used to communicate the seasonal trends. Commentary should include the season's silhouettes, proportions, color, fabrics, accessories, and distinguishable details. Audiences react to color more readily than other elements of design and it is often a starting point when delivering commentary.

Commentary should go from general information about the garment or trends to specific information about a detail. It should allow the audience to travel with the trends from item to item showing congruity between outfits. Notice the transition for conventional dressing to contemporary dressing in the following example:

Suiting up for spring may include a traditional gray, checked ensemble, but throw in a twist of color. Notice the polka-dot pocket square. A big trend of dots, large and small, is here to stay for the spring.

Customers are often equally concerned for function and fashion. Fabric details may be examples of function as in the following:

Terrycloth because of its looped structure is one of the most absorbent textures in the world. This "pretty in pink" robe will definitely keep you warm and dry after that long, hot shower.

Commentary should not be so detailed that it bores the audience. Never make an audience feel unintelligent by stating every detail that they can easily see. If it is necessary to make an obvious statement, use a trendy term or color to add information to the statement. For example a fashion color such as "rich, cranberry red" may inform the audience of something trendy for the upcoming season rather that using only "red" to describe a garment. An example of *unacceptable* descriptive commentary follows:

Our next model is wearing a black cardigan suit. The jacket has one button closure, set in sleeves, and shoulder pads. Her matching 24" long slim skirt has tunnel belt and a back zipper. This dry-cleanable rayon is imported. The white blouse with a draped, cross-over, V-neckline has a concealed button front. This polyester blouse is machine washable.

An audience appreciates hearing a designer discuss his or her own collection. Albert Nipon responds to audience questions.

Overly opinionated and superlative words are also undesirable in commentary. Descriptive words that mean nothing such as ravishing, adorable, and glamorous should not be written into the commentary. The audience should be able to make up their minds without editorial remarks from the commentator. Another example of *unacceptable* opinionated commentary follows:

Our next spectacular model looks fabulous in this superb, cardigan suit. The alluring jacket and skirt sets this model apart from the rest of the crowd. Just look at those precious adornments.

Good commentary can be developed from these unacceptable examples. Keeping in mind that commentary provides information about the trends of the season, new details, and the current color palette, an *acceptable* commentary describing this outfit is rewritten in the following paragraph:

This season the businesswoman reflects the image of Chanel with her cardigan suit. The skirt length represents the latest proportions for career dressing. The rayon suit is versatile and easy to care for. The cranberry quilted handbag and spectator shoes complement the Chanel influence.

Words To Avoid Certain terms have become trite and should not be used in commentary such as ever-popular, style show or any sexist terms like housewife. Cute, delightful or wonderful are gushy adjectives that do not add anything to the commentary and should be avoided. Overusing terms or icons from popular culture detracts from the commentary.

Using Prices in the Commentary The type of fashion show and audience will determine whether or not to include the price of apparel or accessories in the written commentary. Prices may be included in the program or occasionally mentioned in the commentary. Many individuals feel the amount they spend on clothing is personal. The audience would be interested in price if the product is an exceptionally good value. However, excessive use of prices in commentary becomes monotonous. Price may also be mentioned for its shock value. Price points may be essential information in a show with the primary purpose of selling goods such as wearable art or luxury items.

Using a Model's Name in the Commentary Whether or not to use a model's name is determined by the type of show and audience. Trade shows and shows using professional models do not incorporate the model's name into the commentary. In most instances, the commentator should address the models in a formal manner, avoiding calling models by their first names or making personal references to certain models. This gives a more professional look to the show. During a very informal show the commentator may be more conversational in approach to the models and call them by name. Civic or school shows may use models' names in the commentary to recognize the contributions of amateur models. At a recent show, a commentator, who was the designer of a line of Native American fashions, made a point of calling each model by name and explaining the model's Native American heritage. By using the model's names, the models felt more at ease in displaying their culture and the audience felt more connected with the models in learning about the culture.

Using a Manufacturer's or Designer's Name in the Commentary Identifying the designer or manufacturer is determined by audience awareness and affiliation with the company. Recognized designers or manufacturers names may contribute to increased sales of those goods. Unknown designers or manufacturers mean nothing to the audience and may add confusion.

THE COMMENTATOR

The best commentators are comfortable speaking in front of an audience and have a good working knowledge of current fashion. The commentator must adapt to the type of show being produced and blend into the theme. The commentator should approach the task with utmost professionalism. He or she should be very aware of being in front of an audience and not show any attitude towards the show workings. Commentators must put their egos aside and complement the show.

An experienced commentator can more easily adapt to different types of shows. A commentator should prepare by knowing the current fashion looks, terminology, and colors for the season. He or she must also know which fibers and accessories to promote and demonstrate expertise about fashion to the audience.

Models and the commentator must work together very closely to execute entrances and exits smoothly. The models should be informed ahead of time as to what type of commentary will be used and what kind of cues will be used. Certain shows are staged with continuous commentary regardless of when a model enters the stage. Other shows are performed with commentary recited as the model enters the stage. It is the task of the commentator to not bring mistakes of the models to the attention of the audience. If an obvious mistake does occur that cannot be overlooked the commentator must be gracious to the model and be poised throughout the situation.

On occasion a celebrity may be asked to commentate a show. They are usually brought in to add significance to the show and draw a larger audience. Be careful when selecting a

Qualities of a Good Commentator

Comfortable as a public speaker
Good knowledge of current fashion terminology
Ability to make the audience feel at ease
Professional in actions and appearance
Not place oneself above the designs being shown
Iillustrate the store philosophy in dress and appearance
Complement the theme of the show
Not be flamboyant or overstated in appearance
Neat in makeup, nails and grooming

Qualities of a Good Commentator

A *Glamour* editor points out "dos and don'ts of fashion."

celebrity that he or she is knowledgeable of fashion and is willing to cooperate with show personnel, not placing themselves above the fashions being presented at the show.

The Commentator's Appearance

The dress and appearance of the commentator must express her fashion expertise without being too flamboyant. The models are on stage not the commentator. The dress of the commentator should complement the theme of the show if appropriate. If the commentator is a representing a retail store, the store's philosophy must be obvious in the appearance of the commentator. If the theme does not lend itself to be used by the commentator then the commentator should dress in classic, understated clothing not drawing attention away from the garments on stage. Hair, makeup, and nails should also be appropriate to the show without upstaging the hair or makeup of the models on stage. Current accessories should be worn by the commentator as long as they do not interfere with the microphone.

Number of Commentators

Most shows use one commentator. If the show is lengthy and two people can easily work together, a pair of commentators may be used. In a school production co-commentators help each other to overcome nerves and stage fright. Another variation to commentary may be to use an emcee or announcer as a master of ceremonies, making the audience feel comfortable during intermissions. Using an emcee and a commentator allows for both the audience and the commentators to experience variations in speaking styles.

It is important that the commentator understand the sophistication of the audience when writing commentary. Very sophisticated audiences require very little commentary because they can interpret the fashion statements. Less sophisticated audiences need more detail within the commentary to make sure the fashion statements are understood. Further details of the audience may be influential when formulating commentary including age, sex, nationality, or other features. Galeries Lafayette, a Paris retailer known for their weekly fashion shows for foreign tourists, knows ahead of show time the nationalities of the audience so that they may have commentary prepared in the various languages. Commentary is regularly available in English, Italian, French, Spanish, and Japanese. Other languages are available on request.

The use of commentary must be carefully considered when producing a fashion show. Used ineffectively commentary can lose an audience in the first few minutes of the show. Used effectively commentary can sell the fashions.

KEY FASHION SHOW TERMS

commentary	filler commentary	partial commentary
commentary card	full commentary	script commentary
commentator	impromptu commentary	

ADDITIONAL READINGS

1. Corinth, *Fashion Showmanship* (1970): Commentator and Commentary (Chapter 11).

2. Diehl, *How to Produce a Fashion Show* (1976): Commentator and Commentary (Chapter 8).

3. Guerin, *Fashion Writing* (1972): Fashion Shows (Chapter 6).

9

Staging Framework

Setting the atmosphere for the presentation comes together in the staging framework—the layout of the physical facilities. The general architectural limitations for the staging and background for the show depend on the type of show being presented and the location chosen. An informal modeling of fashions in a restaurant or tea room will not require any special physical staging considerations. Attention to mobile props may be sufficient. A large production show may require a great deal of concentration on staging and background effects. Shows produced in an apparel market center may be limited by the physical layout provided by the mart for such productions. A theater may provide various elevated runways. These may be constructed in a number of different configurations, depending upon the size of the audience and room capacity.

A particular designer may wish to emphasize certain images or illusions. The fashion presentations in Paris are particularly known for their theatrical staging and backdrops *(Balavender, 1990)*. Some specific examples include the following:

- During a fashion show for the House of Chanel, models came onto the stage through a 15-foot quilted handbag. The association of this fashion accessory to Chanel was reinforced when it was used as an architectural backdrop.
- Designer Chantal Thomas created a runway reminiscent of an imaginary ski chalet in the Alps. The white runway was decorated with Victorian gingerbread trim. To emphasize this reproduction of an Alps scene, a staged snow storm was generated during a segment of the show.
- Yohji Yamamoto, a minimalist designer, projected his image through his staging. He constructed a spartan set with a narrow, unfinished wooden runway, reinforcing the austere purity of his designs.

The style of the stage, backdrops, runway, lighting, and props can enhance the environment, helping promote the theme and enjoyment by the audience.

STAGE AND RUNWAYS

The stage is the background area where the models typically enter and exit. The runway, or catwalk as it is called in England, is an extension of the stage or a freestanding unit that generally projects into the audience. It varies according to the needs of the show produced and physical facilities.

A rough sketch and/or floor plan of the design and layout of the stage and runway should be drawn to give the show personnel a general idea of the layout, physical impression, dimensions, and distance from the dressing room to the stage and runway. This information will assist the model, merchandise and choreography committees in planning the timing of the show.

Depending upon the client's request and to help the designer, manufacturer or sponsoring group envision the layout, an artist's perspective rendering may be drawn or three-dimensional scale model may be constructed. Both the drawings and the model will accentuate lighting and provide dramatic views of the stage setting and backdrops. Many professional fashion show producers do not need to invest in these additional expenses. For individuals who are inexperienced in fashion show production this may help in visualizing the area and coordinating different aspects of the show. It will especially assist in planning entrances and exits of the models and timing.

Runways vary in both size and height. When deciding on the type of runway to use, show planners must consider:

- Timing for models to enter the show area from the dressing area
- Walking route and traffic flow
- Height, size and shape as it relates to the room and audience visibility

Regarding timing, the pattern and route the model follows should allow enough time to present the garment to the audience and for the audience to react, but not be bored. The pace should be quick enough to provide interest, without being drawn out too long. The length of the runway also contributes to this aspect.

The distance of the dressing room to the runway should not be ignored. The show coordinator should examine the physical layout of the area and know the proximity of the dressing and stage areas. In an ideal setting the dressing area and the stage are adjacent to one another, which eliminates the need for additional models to compensate for time lost traveling to the stage from the dressing area. The model area needs to be close enough to make rapid changes. One fashion show location site offered a changing room on a different floor from the audience, which was not acceptable to the show production staff. This problem was solved by adapting a room for the models' dressing area near the presentation. Ingenuity with screens, tables, and rolling racks can make even an empty corner on the show floor a suitable dressing room.

One of the most important details in staging is audience visibility. It is essential that the models be seen from every seat in the audience. Attention to pillars, curtains or other archi-

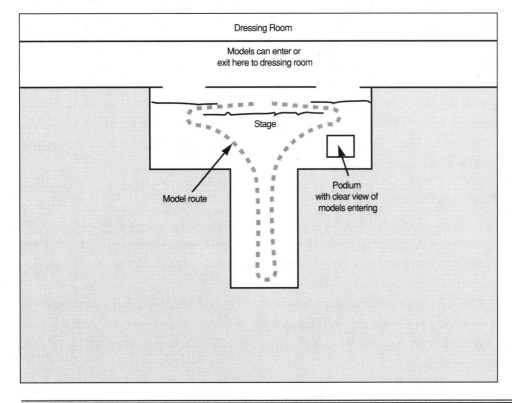

Figure 9-1
General Floor Plan

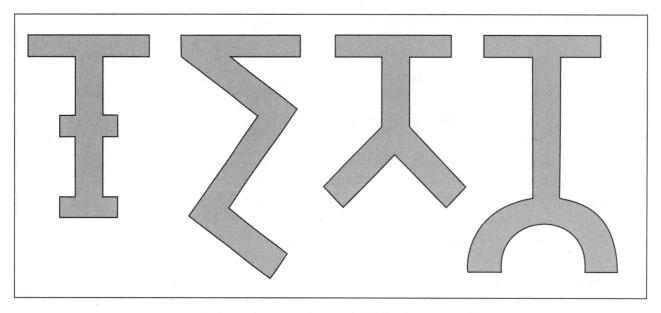

Figure 9-2
Examples of Runway
Shapes

tectural obstructions must be noted. While plants may offer a natural earthy feeling, they should not obstruct the audience view.

The height of the runway should increase the ability of the viewers to see the performance without being so high as to make viewing difficult. The height of the elevation may be dependent upon the height of the stage. Shows presented in small spaces designated specifically for fashion show production such as the showroom at Galeries Lafayette in Paris may have a low elevation of about eight to ten inches. Other shows presented in apparel market theaters may have platforms elevated to 36 or 48 inches. Ideal heights are between 18 and 36 inches.

Since runways are often constructed from plywood, measuring 4 feet by 8 feet, runways are frequently multiples of these measurements. Typical trade show runways are 32 to 40 feet in length. This provides adequate space for models to exhibit the clothing and also allows enough time for the audience to review the line.

The width of the runway will determine the number of models who may appear side by side at any given time. If the runway is four feet wide, only two models should be walking together. The width of the runway may be doubled by putting two sections side by side. When the runway is six feet or eight feet wide, three or four models can be comfortable walking en masse, adding visual impact.

Runway Shapes

The actual runway may be built in a variety of shapes, but the most common configurations include the T, I, X, H, Y, U or Z. The primary limitation to runway design is the size of the auditorium, restaurant, sales floor, or other fashion show locations. There are some advantages and disadvantages to the various runway patterns.

One of the most frequently used runway shapes is the T shape, which is a combination of a stage and an extended runway. Models enter and exit from the stage and walk down the straight platform to exhibit the clothes. It is the most simple runway shape and perhaps the least exciting.

A variation of the basic T shape is the I formation. This runway shape adds a platform extension to the extended runway, parallel to the stage. This extension allows models to spend more time on the runway, closer to the audience to feature the garments in a more interesting manner.

The X or cross shape runway is a unique and fascinating formation, consisting of two platforms that are placed at 90 degree angles, generally used without a stage. This is a unique and fascinating formation. Two or four sets of steps alongside the runway for models to get onto the runway add to their routines. Models enter and exit from doors in the room or auditorium, bringing them closer to the audience.

The H shape runway combines two straight runways with a connecting strip. The advantage of this type of formation is in promoting several models at the same time, and may be effective in creating interest and variety. It is also useful in holding the audience's attention, particularly with large shows. Two successful examples of the use of the H shape runway involve, French ready-to-wear designer, Sonia Rykiel, and the late American designer, Rudi Gernreich. Since the H shape runway can handle many models at the same time and to focus attention on her simple houndstooth suits, Rykiel brought out twelve models identically dressed in the outfit. The Fashion Group of Los Angeles used an H-shaped runway to stage a Rudi Gernreich retrospective show. The runway was so large that it incorporated three separate focal points. The models entered undetected from a secret pathway underneath the stage onto a raised platform, placed in the center of the large stage.

The Y and U patterns are very similar to each other. The Y shape has two angled projections from the basic runway. The U shape has a curved extension, which brings the models out into the audience using a philosophy similar to the "theater in the round." These formations can also be very engaging and add diversity to a show.

The Z or zigzag configuration is a simple yet complex shape conducive to a collection of different routines and movements. The models can turn and change direction to effectively show different views of the garment.

The surface of the runway is another important consideration for the show planner. A carpeted or non-slip surface will help to protect models and shoes. The outside of the runway may be finished with construction materials or covered with fabric tucked or pleated and tacked into place. Another type of covering is a vinyl fabric, which can be used on top of the runway and on the sides. An attractive runway can enhance the theme as well as the image of the location.

THE DRESSING AREA

The dressing area should be large enough to accommodate clothing racks, accessories tables, chairs, full-length mirrors, the number of models, and the necessary support personnel. Clothing needs to be spaced on the racks to prevent wrinkling and allow easy access by the dressers. One mirror must be placed at the end so models can get a last-minute check before leaving the dressing area. If the auditorium or hotel does not have mirrors, the fashion show producers should make arrangements to have them at the site. The dressing room

Figure 9-3

Dressing Room Supply List

SUPPLIES NEEDED

Office Supplies
_____ Tape
_____ Stapler
_____ Pens/Pencils
_____ Paper
_____ Garment tags

Alterations Supplies
_____ Needles
_____ Safety pins/Straight pins
_____ Thread
_____ Scissors

Beauty Supplies
_____ Anti-perspirant
_____ Dress shields
_____ Hair pins/hair elastics
_____ Brushes/combs
_____ Hair spray/mousse
_____ Makeup: eyeshadows, blush, lipstick
_____ Nail polish

Equipment
_____ Extension cords
_____ Mirrors
_____ Tables / racks / chairs
_____ Iron / ironing board / steamer

Miscellaneous Supplies
_____ Stockings
_____ Floor coverings
_____ Hangers
_____ First-aid kit

must be clean and free of unnecessary clutter. All unnecessary chairs and props should be removed to allow people to more around freely.

The show coordinator should plan the organization of the dressing area. The type of show, the number of models and dressers, and the size of the room will determine this organization. Each model should have an assigned space in the dressing area. The spaces should be assigned according to the models' order in the show. To avoid cluttering the space, models who appear together in the show should not have to dress in the same space. Model's clothing and accessories should be placed in this area. If a model has several changes they should be in order to help changes move more smoothly. If there is only one table for accessories, it should be placed next to the exit so the accessories will be the last items a model puts on. Space should be reserved for models to apply makeup or style their hair or for makeup artists and hair stylists. The dressing area should have a clearly defined entrance and exit to prevent awkward movements that may be seen by the audience.

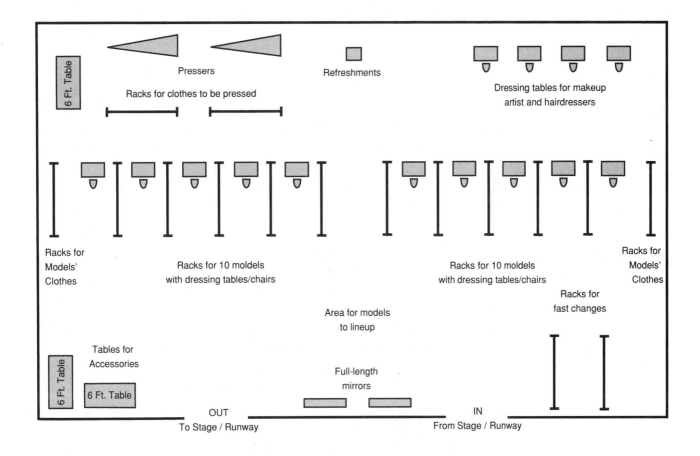

Figure 9-4

This floor plan can be used to layout a dressing area for approximately 20 models and 80 outfits.

BACKGROUNDS

The purpose of the background is to enhance the products shown, either with stark settings emphasizing the garments or dramatic backdrops emphasizing the theme or classification of merchandise being presented. It may be decorated with a designer's, retailer's, or manufacturer's logo or some type of scenic theme.

Currently the trend in fashion shows is to use simple backgrounds. The simplest backdrop is a frame or doorway. The frame may be designed using a gazebo, trellis or column structure that will also serve as an entry for the models. Large potted plants or architectural boxes or pillars can also frame an entrance and serve this purpose.

Another popular type of entryway consists of a plain white panel or screen, normally seven to eight feet tall and ten to twelve feet wide. Slides can be projected onto this screen to emphasize a particular theme or information. Interesting accents can be developed with video walls. The screen may be used as a background for dramatic lighting and shadow effects created for the beginning or ending of a fashion show segment. The show planners may have the option of permanent or temporary movable backdrops called flats.

Scenery, just like a theatrical stage backdrop, may be painted to represent a room setting or an outdoor scene with natural elements. A series of doors or panels through which the models enter the stage and runway area can also be designed.

The extent of the backdrop and scenery are dependent upon the type of show and the budget planned. A single backdrop can be used for the entire show or different and elaborate backdrops can be built for each scene of the show, such as a revolving stage to change the scene for each show segment. With a more elaborate stage setting the expense is greater. The staging should never overshadow the clothes. It should be used to flatter what is being displayed.

Decorative elements may be used to enhance the theme and atmosphere as part of the stage set. A Native American show featured colorful dried corn, baskets and native plants combined with Navajo rugs and cradle boards to emphasize the ethnic heritage of the models and merchandise. Texas has always taken great pride in the ranching, farming, and agricultural heritage of the region. Fashion show planners could display this pride through the use of spurs, ropes, saddles, and other Western decor on the stage. A large map of Texas would, of course, be the backdrop for such a show.

The merchandise itself can be used to create a dramatic effect for the show opening. In April 1988 Isaac Mizrahi let the merchandise create the explosive mood. The first models came onto the runway wearing neutral-colored clothing. International model Linda Evangelista shattered the mood by stepping out onto the runway wearing a bright orange coat. This unexpected explosion of vibrant color led to an outburst from the excited audience.

PROPS

Props are supports used to highlight the garments being exhibited. The trend for using props is cyclical. Sometimes it is popular to use props and at other times show planners want the clothes to speak for themselves.

Props may be mobile or stationary. Carrying a tennis racquet or golf club with the appropriate apparel are examples of movable props. There are a wide variety of such types of props including: jump ropes and hand weights with activewear, briefcases and newspapers with career apparel, beach balls and towels with swimwear, a notebook or apple with back-to-school fashions. Merchandise available for sale such as the briefcase or school bookbag may be used as props.

Stationary props are generally immobile items. They are placed as part of the scenery. These items might include furniture for a room setting, one or two beach umbrellas for a swimwear segment, a motorcycle or car for a teen or menswear show, a gazebo for a bridal show. Although these props are typically heavy and bulky, they could be changed with scene changes.

SEATING PATTERNS

There are two styles of seating arrangements to accommodate the audience. They may be seated in a theater pattern or at tables.

Tables are placed surrounding the runway. Seats provide the best possible viewing while accommodating food service.

Theater Seating

Theater seating involves placing chairs side by side and next to the stage and runway and is best used for fashion shows without meal service. The audience may have assigned or open seating on a first come first served basis. Programs, gifts or promotional materials may be placed on the seats before the patrons arrive. Theater seating generally provides the best view of the show pieces since all the members of the audience are seated facing the runway.

Table Seating

A table seating arrangement is used at a show with some sort of meal service. A buffet or sit down meal could be served prior to or after the fashion show. There are some visibility problems with this type of seating. Often a round table is set, holding as many as eight to ten people. Some people will not be able to see the stage or runway. Chairs will have to be turned in order to fully view the presentation and some members of the audience may find this kind of seating awkward.

Combination Seating

Depending upon the location, available space and budget a group may combine both seating styles. The lunch or dinner could be served in one banquet room using a table seating. After the meal the audience could move to another location where the stage, runway, and theater seating are set up.

LIGHTING

Good lighting is necessary to show clothing to its best advantage, to set the mood of the show, and to accentuate the theme of the show. Raising and lowering the house lights adds to the theatrical nature of fashion shows. Spotlights or track lighting placed above the runway can be used to highlight the models while they are on the runway. Spotlights in a darkened room can be used to introduce, emphasize or close a segment. Spotlights should be located as high as possible. They should not "blind" the audience.

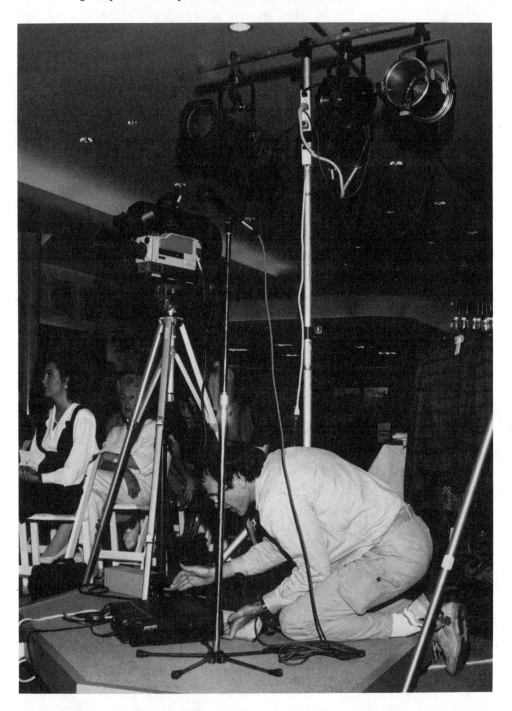

Technicians make adjustments for video taping and appropriate lighting.

There may be limited lighting in the area where the garments are shown. One fashion show held in the carriage house of a historical site had virtually no lights over the area where the runway was placed. Photographer's spotlights were used to illuminate the modeling area.

Strobe lights were popular effects used to create a mechanical look during the 1960s. In the 1970s and 1980s such theatrical productions as *Phantom of the Opera*, *Cats*, and *Starlight Express* created by Andrew Lloyd Weber led to dramatic lighting and staging effects. These influences can be seen in some of the more complex and expensive fashion shows held during this period.

Many designers incorporate colored lights into their shows. Colored gels have been used to accentuate a particular look. A recent fashion presentation produced by Enrico Coveri used pink runways and to further enhance this look added pink-gelled lamps. Along with his colorful and youth collection, the presentation popped!

Care and practice with lighting should take place before the show to prevent any potential lighting problems. Lighting cues should be practiced during rehearsals.

The atmosphere of a show is largely determined through the appropriate use of the physical facilities and effective use of the staging framework. The stage or runway, background, props, seating, and lighting must be planned and coordinated for the most striking and successful presentation to excite an audience and to generate sales.

KEY FASHION SHOW TERMS

background	runway	table seating
lighting	stage	theater seating
prop		

ADDITIONAL READINGS

1. Balavender, R., (July 1990): "Clues from the Collections," *Visual Merchandising & Store Design* (pp 18-22).

2. Corinth, *Fashion Showmanship* (1970): How to Put Showmanship into the Fashion Show (Chapter 7).

3. Diehl, *How to Produce a Fashion Show* (1976): Setting up for the Show: The Floor Plan (Chapter 9).

4. Guerin, *Creative Fashion Presentations* (1987): the runway (pp 159-162).

10

Choreography

Choreography refers to the art of devising movements for dances such as classical or modern ballet or musical show performances. This term is used in the broadest sense for fashion show production. Fashion show choreography includes the plan for the models' walking or dancing runway routines as well as any specific dance numbers. The theme, merchandise, and music selected are elements that reflect the look and feel of the show and the choreography should enhance this image.

PATTERNS OF CHOREOGRAPHY

Choreography is an important aspect of a fashion show and is often overlooked by inexperienced show planners. Models should not be expected to just enter and walk down the runways at random. All their runway routines for the show should be worked out before they arrive for the rehearsal. Models will either be posed on stage as the curtain opens or enter quickly and assume a place on cue. The traveled patterns will ensure that the appropriate commentary is emphasized on cue. A choreographer is responsible for determining the pattern that a model will travel down the runway and the interaction of the models on the runway as they enter and exit the stage area. A large show may use an individual choreographer for these routines. Other shows may rely on the fashion director to give the models their cues.

Choreography need not be expensive. Simple routines that are repeated will keep the costs low. Choreography becomes expensive when more elaborate dance numbers are included, and when it becomes necessary to pay professional dancers to learn, rehearse and perform production numbers.

Patterns of choreography include:
- Opening the show and entering the stage
- Planning paces, pivots and poses on the stage and runway
- Exiting the stage and/or runway

Opening the Show

Perhaps the most important part of show choreography is the opening. It is critical to the success of the show to get the audience involved right from the beginning. The house lights are dark. A spotlight is focused on one model at the stage entrance. As the general lighting is raised, the model or models enter the runway. The merchandise, music, lighting, and choreography must all come together. There is a significant difference between the fashion show and a theatrical performance. A theatrical performance may open slowly and quietly and build to a climax and conclusion. A fashion show must start and end with emphasis. For example a very effective entrance for a fashion show with an active or casual theme may involve several models wearing similar styles in different colors coming onto the stage to some dance number. Four or five models wearing leotards doing an exercise routine to some upbeat music is bound to grab the attention of the viewer. The choreographer may plan an entrance that would give the illusion of going to work on a subway or train and bring out a group of male and female models dressed in business apparel.

Another possible show opening may involve some type of visual effects on the background such as a slide, video or a light show while the models enter onto the stage. This can

Dancing models such as this one for Courrèges became the norm in the 1960s couture shows. (Bruce Davidson/Magnum Photos)

also be used to entertain and perhaps educate the audience before the models come on the runway. Each scene of the show may open using a technique similar to the one used in opening the overall presentation.

Pace, Pivots, and Poses

The choreographer will give the models specific directions regarding the pace of the show, where pivots and pauses should take place on the runway. Although it is the easiest to have each model enter, pivot, pause, and exit in the same manner, the audience would become too bored with the show. There should be some variety in the pattern and model routines to interest the audience. The choreographer may chose to control the model's pivots and poses, and actually determine where they will take place on the runway. For example a simple plan may be to use three or four different routines.

Mapping

It is not necessary to create a different route for each model as he or she demonstrates each new outfit. It would be difficult for the models and choreographer to remember each separate walk. A compromise of approximately four to eight routes could be mapped in advance, and will allow for some variability. Then as models are given directions, these mapped routes, planned paths, can be explained and presented as visual diagrams. This number of variations will not be too confusing for the models or show personnel to remember. The route can be numbered and the number posted with each model's outfit in the dressing room.

Dancing

Dancing routines can add a great deal of interest to the show. During the 1960s and 1970s dancing took on a new and engaging impact on fashion show production. Professionally trained dancers can easily pick up the routines during the rehearsal. Amateurs may require an additional rehearsal to learn, practice, and become comfortable with the routines.

Showing a dress with fringe may be complemented by doing a simple Charleston. Evening clothes may be emphasized by a waltz or tango. Large production numbers could be used to emphasize a particular look or theme.

Dance numbers may be used between the various scenes of a show, such as between scenes of workout wear and business attire, to allow models more time to change. A Native American dancer provided entertainment between segments of a show featuring southwestern fashions. The dancer emphasized the theme of the show while models had extra changing time.

Model Groups

A simple parade of models walking on the runway, one after the other can be boring. It generally adds more interest and variety when the show is broken up with different patterns and groupings. Two models entering the runway wearing the same or complementary outfits creates greater impact and the repetition will help the audience remember the look.

Variations using multiple models are endless. It is common to have two, three, four or more models on the runway at any given time. The show will be more complex in staging, but it will be more entertaining and effective in showing different colors and designs to the audience. A greater number of models will require more coordination in fittings and rehearsal.

When working with two or more models, the model on the left is considered the lead model. Stage left is considered the left part of the stage from the viewpoint of the audience facing the stage. The other models should keep pace with the lead model. Followers need to practice when to start, turn and stop in relationship to the lead model.

Two models together may walk to the center of the runway. At the point where a pause or pivot takes place, these two models may make simultaneous turns and continue or separate, walking in different directions. Planning choreography in advance will ease the transitions. When three models come on stage together, an effective choreography method is to have all three models pose together on the center stage. Then the center model moves away and walks to the middle of the runway, called the pivot point. As she turns, the other two models walk to the pivot point. They pass the center model, turn at the pivot point, and continue to the end of the runway. The center model may return to the center of the runway, meeting the other models as they return. All three models return to the exit point, leaving the stage one at a time.

Be careful during the merchandise selection process and coordination of amateur models into groups. Keep in mind the model, his or her grouping, and the merchandise he or she will wear—the models may not look good together on the runway. One fashion show featured the same horizontally striped dress on a petite, curvy figured model and on a tall slender model. The coordinator tried to make the point of featuring the same dress in the different complementary colors. Each individual model looked wonderful in the dress.

A fashion show is more interesting when model groupings or pairs are used in addition to single models.

However the effect that the coordinator wanted to create was not flattering to such distinct body types. It created a negative rather than positive impact.

"The show must go on," is one important point to emphasize with amateur models. Despite elaborate planning and rehearsal, the model may forget the exact route. It is more important to show the garments in a professional manner than to act confused trying to figure out what to do next. If the model who forgets some part of the choreography remembers to smile warmly, the audience is likely to be forgiving.

EXITING THE STAGE

As the model leaves the runway or stage, he or she may stop, turn, pause and pose, enabling the audience to take one last view of the item being presented. The model's personal flair may be revealed with some special pose or exit. It will also give a photographer time to take another photograph.

The plan must include directions for the models who are simultaneously entering and exiting the stage area. It must be determined if the first model will remain on the runway while the second model enters.

Galeries Lafayette used a unique method to cue models for their exit. Stagelights were dimmed briefly as a signal for the models to leave the runway. A technician who could view both the runway and backstage could see when the next model was ready. This simple yet effective indication allowed for a smooth transition of the models on and off stage without being obvious to the audience.

THE FINALE

The end of every show should be well coordinated and powerful. It should leave the audience happy and applauding. The finale is the last impression.

Generally the merchandise in the final scene is dramatic in nature. It may be elegant hostess apparel, evening clothes or bridal fashions. The most effortless ending is to bring all of the models, wearing their final outfit, back on stage. By bringing all of the models back on the runway, the audience is able to review the most spectacular clothing shown during the performance. This type of finale benefits from a large number of models, who by their presence on the runway provides dramatic impact. Each model can be positioned along the runway. Models may pivot and leave on cue as individuals or as a group.

Special stage sets may be used to emphasize the finale. A stained glass window could be used as a prop for a wedding scene. A gazebo with distinctive lighting could be used as a tableau. Furniture and background posters may symbolize a room setting.

One basic rule of thumb in planning the show finale is to save the best for last. The garments should be selected with this in mind. The category or theme of merchandise for the final scene may suggest some creative finale, such as carrying balloons, tossing streamers or confetti for a celebration or holiday theme.

When a show features designs from a celebrity designer, it is customary to have the celebrity join the models on stage during the finale. The show may be a charity event or a retail store promotion where potential customers like to see and meet the creator of the garments. Personal appearances by the designer are very popular events for retail stores. If the show is held during market week, buyers and media personnel wish to recognize the achievements of the designer's work as part of the finale.

Models wearing the last outfit go back stage and bring the designer out on the runway. The models are applauding the designer, the designer recognizes his or her models, fashion show staff and audience by clapping for them. The audience is also likely to applaud the show and designer.

IMPORTANCE OF CHOREOGRAPHY

Properly organized and performed choreography can be used to create focal points for the show. The viewer's attention is drawn to the specific merchandise or trends that the show producers want to emphasize. A poorly choreographed show looks amateurish and unprofessional, and does not leave a good impression on the audience.

Choreography should be appropriate for the type of show being produced and the audience. Up-to-the minute dance routines will interest a younger audience. Ballroom dancing would appeal to a mature audience. The type of dancing or walking planned for the choreography can be used to reflect the interests and experience of the audience.

Choreography can be used to reveal certain moods. Elegant and sophisticated merchandise may be accentuated through slow deliberate movements and dramatic pauses. Athletic

Variety can be achieved by placing models at different locations on the stage and runway.

apparel can be highlighted through spirited and energetic gestures. Children's apparel can be stressed through skipping, running, playing games and so forth. The viewers should be entertained and satisfied with the show so that they will support the mission of the program, whether it is for charity or profit.

KEY FASHION SHOW TERMS

choreography	mapped route	pause
dancing	model group	pivot
finale	pace	

ADDITIONAL READINGS

1. Lenz, *The New Complete Guide of Fashion Modeling* (1982).

11

Music

The first retailer to set fashion shows to music was Stanley Marcus who in the 1920s used the Ted Weems band as background music for his weekly fashion shows *(Diehl, 1976)*. Many other retailers readily adapted this feature and today **music** is the vocal and instrumental sound environment used by fashion show producers to heighten the atmosphere of the show for the audience. Many contemporary designers feel that, "...the right music is essential to the success of the show." *(Boyes, 1990, p. 26)* The right music can get an audience excited about what they are going to see more rapidly than any other element of the preshow ambience. Trade shows rely exclusively on music to create the mood and emotions of the show because they do not use commentary.

Music is available as taped or live, vocals or instrumental. Blues, classical, contemporary, jazz, new age, rap, reggae, and rock music are all successful in influencing an audience. However, it is extremely important that the music selected be pleasant to the intended audience. Teenagers may be turned off by classical orchestras while their parents may be turned off by hard rock bands. Music should match the tastes of the audience. For example an organization such as a symphony guild may incorporate a live string quartet for entertainment and background. A group so closely aligned with music should make this an integral part of the event.

Models depend on music to set the pace of the show. They listen to the music and can more easily move in rhythmic dancing rather than in a straight walk on the stage. If the music has a fast beat, models will walk faster which may then require more outfits to fill the show time properly. This should be a factor when selecting music and merchandise.

Music directors and fashion designers work very closely in planning music for the show. *(WWD)*

MUSIC DIRECTOR

The **music director** will research and select the appropriate music, obtain permissions to use copyrighted music, mix the music at the show, and prepare the sound system at the show site. The use of music may be limited to the show itself, or played as background as the audience enters the show site. Silence in a room can frequently make people feel uncomfortable about talking or moving around before the show begins. Soft music playing as background will make an audience feel more comfortable and at ease about being at the show.

For most fashion shows, music directors or technicians are hired to play taped music during the show and occasionally they may be asked to prepare the music. The music director may be a professional affiliated with the location selected for the fashion show or a free lance technician. Local theaters and auditoriums often have their own technical staff who know the specifics of the equipment at that location. Although these technicians are provided by the facility, the fashion show producer must pay their wages for working the show. A music technician, an expert in musical styles and sound systems, is more aware of problems that can occur with the sound system and can make any needed corrections. Technicians should attend all rehearsals in which music is needed to note cues from the commentator and the models.

Figure 11-1

Music Planning Sheet

MERCHANDISE CATEGORIES & MUSICAL SELECTION	RECORDING ARTIST	LENGTH OF SELECTION
"Good Mornin"'		
Morning Has Broken	Cat Stevens	1:11
Good Morning Vietnam	Robin Williams	0:38
My Baby Takes the Morning Train	Sheena Easton	3:49
Rise and Shine	Harry Belafonte	2:54
Wake Up	The Everly Brothers	4:15
"Workin' Overtime"		
Working Overtime	Aretha Franklin	3:51
Working 9 to 5	Dolly Parton	3:44
Working for a Living	Huey Lewis & The News	4:57
Wild Women Do	Natalie Cole	4:06
Here Comes The Sun	Beatles	3:25
"Going Through the Motions"		
Footloose	Kenny Loggins	4:52
Savannah's Song	Yaz	6:01
Pump It Up	L.L.Cool J.	5:22
Burnin' Up	Madonna	4:55
Jump	The Pointer Sisters	3:36
How Many Times	Erasure	5:10
"You Can Leave Your Hat On"		
Leave Your Hat On	Joe Cocker	4:33
Relax	Frankie Goes To Hollywood	5:45
December	George Winston	4:34
Song Bird	Fleetwood Mac	3:28
Dock of The Bay	Michael Bolton	5:31
Silhouette	Kenny G	4:09
"Girls Just Want to Have Fun"		
Wanna Have Fun	Cyndi Lauper	4:02
Party	Madonna	4:18
She Bop	Cyndi Lauper	3:32
Real Wild One	Iggy Pop	4:44
When The Night Comes	Joe Cocker	5:10
Love Street	World Party	3:51

MUSIC MIX

Music mix is the combination of different musical styles to create a specified mood. The music should match the commentary and the merchandise, starting with a strong musical selection to capture the attention of the audience and finishing with a finale that they will remember. The middle segments of the show should have music that flows so easily that the audience is unaware that they are listening to anything. Isaac Mizrahi always starts his shows with a show tune because he says, "I like the grandness and the swelling of the music... it's purely entertainment." *(Boyes, page 26, 1990)*

A designer show presenting Native American fashions complemented the ethnic designs with the music selections. The first selection starting the show was a traditional ethnic piece using native flute and drum instruments. The audience immediately noticed the Native American fashions displayed. The music flowed into the music of Dan Fogelberg, maintaining the soft mood. The next piece blended into light country rock, the beat increasing in momentum as the fashions became more creative to excite the audience. The show finished with the harder country rock music of Jimmy Buffet as a finale of the most spectacular fashions of the evening were presented. All the music selections were mixed so smoothly that the audience was not aware of the added momentum in the beat of the music.

A careful match is a necessity if music is to be used productively. A variety of music should be used. Music that is appropriate to the audience may become monotonous if there is not enough variety in the selections. Ideally, each scene should have music specifically mixed for its merchandise selection. Sportswear requires fast tempo, upbeat music while eveningwear requires slower, sophisticated, subtle music. Youth shows require music that the audience will immediately recognize and identify with. When planning music for the show many songs will be reviewed to match the merchandise grouping.

The Planning Sheet

It is important to list all of the selections that may be appropriate for the show on the planning sheet. The title of the song, the recording artist, and the length of the song are included. The initial list will have more selections then will be actually used. Music edited for the final show will be slightly longer than the length of the show.

LIVE VERSUS TAPED MUSIC

It should be determined whether live or taped music will be used. Each form has benefits and detriments which should be evaluated before a decision is made.

Live music is music performed by musicians during the show and can provide the personal touch to the show that is lacking with taped music. However live music requires a budget to pay professional musicians for their time, both during the show and at rehearsals. Musicians can be limited to a soloist or a small band to minimize expenses, and still provide diversity within their musical style to avoid monotony in the selections. Although live music may be expensive, the musicians are able to adapt to the pace of the show by viewing the actions on the stage.

Taped music is the more popular mode of accompaniment for fashion shows because of the convenience it provides. Pre-recorded music from records, cassettes, or compact disks (CD's) are copied to a tape to play during the show. Costs involve fees to mix the tape professionally or privately by a knowledgeable committee member. Costs for preparing a tape may range from several hundred dollars to five thousand dollars for sound operation during the show. It is more cost effective than live music because it has a one time cost regardless of the number of rehearsals needed. Taped music allows for the most trendy and familiar songs of the moment to be used adding to the excitement of the audience. Taped music may be able to provide a variety through the use of CD's, cassettes, or records which live musicians may not be able to create. Music for each scene may be completely different to provide added variety.

In order to have smooth transitions between scenes, two systems should be set up to play more than one tape during the show. Music for each scene should be alternately taped on two tapes so that the music may be faded in and out at the proper time. The music for the first, third, fifth, and so forth scenes should be taped onto tape A while the second, forth, sixth, and so forth scenes should be placed on tape B.

At the beginning of a scene the music should fade in, starting very softly and then gradually accelerating to the volume to be used throughout the scene. Fading out the music is used at the end of a scene to reverse the process, gradually lowering the volume of the music until it is inaudible. Unless a dramatic effect is desired, music should not start out loud, for this may startle the audience. Just as variety is required in musical selections, volume of the music should also be varied to avoid monotony. Fading in and out allows for longer or shorter scene transitions as needed by the models or behind the scene staff without making the audience aware of any problems.

Live Mixed Music   An alternative to live or taped music is live mixed music. A disk jockey who uses turntables or other playback equipment is hired to change the music with various segments of the show. It is less expensive than hiring live musicians and timing problems associated with pre-recorded music are eliminated.

Music is selected and timed to match the merchandise. These tapes will be used during a designer's press show. *(WWD)*

VOCAL MUSIC

There is a fine line whether to use vocal music or instrumental music to accompany a fashion show. It was thought in the past to never use vocals because the audience could be distracted by the lyrics. Today, music with vocals is so popular that it is hard to ignore this music when planning a fashion show.

Setting the mood is such a large factor in producing a fashion show that it is important to pay close attention to the words of the music. For example, a vocal, *Leave Your Hat On*, by artist Joe Cocker, was used as background to complement a merchandise category. Similarly the song, *Working Nine to Five*, made popular by Dolly Parton, has become a favorite theme song for business apparel.

Vocals can have a positive or negative influence on a show. If the vocals are popular with the audience they can add familiarity to the show. Caution should be taken not to make the vocals too loud or the audience will tune out the commentary and listen only to the music. Calvin Klein prefers music with vocals and pays attention to every word. He states that, "…you don't want the words to be pretentious or depressing… and you don't want the lyrics to be too strong a statement on your clothes." *(Boyes, 1990)*

SOUND LIBRARY

Music from a sound library should be used when possible because it eliminates the need for copyright permission. A sound library is a collection of records, cassettes, and CD's to be used by the public. Copyright permission is authorization from the owner of the copyright to use copyrighted materials. Permissions from a sound library have already been obtained for use by the general public. In some instances, a tape which will only be used for the fashion show and then destroyed, may not require copyright permission. However, it is best to check with the sound library for necessary permissions.

Copyrighted Music

If a commercial album is used, copyright permission must be obtained. To acquire permission it is necessary to determine who owns the copyright. Usually the record producer or the artist holds the copyright. A letter to the recording company should be sent asking for specific permission to use selected cuts from the album. Permissions may be easier to obtain if the show will not be making a profit for the show producer. It is advisable to allow enough lead time to obtain the necessary permissions before the materials are needed. Ask for permissions as far in advance of the show as possible to guarantee the music chosen can be used at show time. If you do not receive a response to your request for permission, you cannot assume you have been granted the necessary permission. Two other organizations which may provide information about the use of recordings are the *American Society of Composers, Authors, and Publishers*, 1 Lincoln Plaza, New York, New York 10023 and *Broadcast Music Incorporated*, 40 West 57th Street, New York, New York 10019.

Sound technicians work the board at an outdoor fashion show.

SOUND SYSTEM

In addition to preparing music for the fashion show, the music coordinator must arrange to have a sound system and public address system available for the commentator. The **public address system** is the microphone, amplifiers, and speakers. The **sound system** is the equipment needed to play the music, and may include a turntable, cassette player, or CD player; speakers, equalizer, and necessary wiring to allow the sound to be heard at the location. Certain locations will have sound systems available for use. If a sound system is not provided at the site, the components may be rented from local rental companies. The rental fee must be included in the budget. It is important to test the sound system with the music system before rehearsing with the models. Often a technical run-through with lights and sound is necessary to learn cues. If the music or the commentary is inaudible the audience will loose interest in the show. Annoying hums or shrill whistles of microphones will also detract immediately from the fashions of the show.

The response and enthusiasm to a fashion show can be impacted by music more than other theatrical elements. It is a universal language pulling the audience and fashion show participants together. Music creates the mood to further emphasize the fashion statements.

KEY FASHION SHOW TERMS

copyright permission	music director	sound library
instrumental music	music mix	sound system
live mixed music	planning sheet	taped music
live music	public address system	vocal music

ADDITIONAL READINGS

1. Boyes K. (February 25, 1990). "SA's Sound of Music." *Women's Wear Daily.*

12

The Purpose of the Rehearsal

The **rehearsal** is a practice performance, held in private, in preparation for a public performance. The fashion show coordinator takes this opportunity to solve any problems prior to the public presentation of the show. The rehearsal may be a simple run-through or a full dress rehearsal. The **run-through** is a rehearsal of the show sequence and involves showing the models the choreography. The models are not required to wear their clothing assignments for the show. A **dress rehearsal** consists of a walk-through with garment changes. A **full dress rehearsal** is held to check all aspects of the show including timing, music, and all other technical aspects.

The need for a rehearsal is dependent upon the type of show being produced and the type of model, professional or amateur, being used. When to hold the rehearsal is also dependent on the type of show and the number of staff people involved. A rehearsal may take place one week prior to the show, the day before the show, or the day of the show. An elaborate production show may need a rehearsal far ahead of time. A show set in a retail department may be rehearsed immediately prior to show time. Unfortunately during trade or market week shows, models are often booked for several shows each day. In this case there is only time to give simple verbal commands prior to the start of the show.

A full dress rehearsal is ideal to check lighting, music, and overall fashion show coordination. The dress rehearsal will determine the most efficient traffic flow from the dressing area to the stage. Another important reason to hold a dress rehearsal is to determine the timing of the length of the show. The fashion show coordinator should record the actual time of the full dress rehearsal. Knowing how long the dress rehearsal takes will help models set pace and cues.

If the show uses commentary the tentative lineup will help the show commentator prepare the pace of the show. The commentator will have a good feel for how long models

The rehearsal is an opportunity for models and production staff to polish lineup and choreography. Models are given basic directions for pivot and pose locations. Bill Blass (bottom photo, left) oversees the rehearsal for a show of his merchandise. (*WWD*)

need to be on the runway. With a full dress rehearsal, he or she will also be able to identify segments where model changes are taking longer than expected. The commentator has an excellent opportunity to plan how to use the ad-lib comments and fill information about current fashion trends relating to the fashion story being presented.

After the rehearsal any problems are ironed out and the final lineup is established. Copies of the final lineup should be available in the dressing room for the dressers and starters, for the commentator and the models, for the music and lighting technicians, the stage manager, cue personnel, and the show director. The posted lineup will facilitate the changes for all the fashion show personnel. Everyone needs to know what is expected and when.

PLANNING THE REHEARSAL

There are many considerations that must take place prior to the dress rehearsal. First, all the spaces at the fashion show site must be reserved ahead of time including the stage or runway, dressing areas, storage areas, and access to rest rooms. Often there is a cost for reserving certain spaces and these costs must be budgeted for at the onset of the show. Since there are many costs involved with holding a rehearsal, it is necessary to keep the rehearsals short.

When reserving space, time must be allocated before and after the rehearsal to set up and strike the show. The show coordinator should inform all personnel of the designated time of the rehearsal and what time they should arrive. Music technicians and prop personnel may need to arrive earlier to have the stage set and ready when the models arrive.

Clothing and accessories should be organized and labeled in the dressing room before models arrive. All the elements of each outfit, including accessories, should be pulled together for each model and placed in the order they will be worn. Models and dressers can refer to the tentative lineup master list to verify the order and placement in the lineup.

Models also may need to arrive early to examine the merchandise selection to determine the time they will need to change. Professional models are paid for their participation in rehearsals. Therefore planning is necessary to maximize the use of the models.

The first walk-through involves the models wearing their street clothes. The choreographer gives the models directions regarding entrances, groupings, turns, and exits. If the show involves amateur models, the choreographer may also give some modeling tips and techniques. This first walk-through is done without the benefit of commentary, music or lighting. A second walk-through adds these elements. The full dress rehearsal combines all of the elements into a "pre-show" shakedown.

DRESSERS

The dressers play an extremely important behind the scenes role. Their responsibility is to help the models change, avoiding a chaotic scene in the dressing room. Dressers for professional shows are often fashion students looking for experience in fashion show production. No matter how big or small the show, dressers make the show run smoothly.

A floor covering such as this white sheet protects the clothing as models make changes. *(WWD)*

Ideally each model should have a separate dresser. A good dresser can handle more than one model if the changes are not at the same time.

The dresser must be completely familiar with the lineup. Both the dresser and the model must know the order of the garment presentation—exactly what outfit comes first, second, third, and so forth. The model's responsibility for her outfits was previously stated, but the dresser is also responsible for getting the clothes ready to be worn. Zippers are unzipped, buttons are unbuttoned, tags are hidden. Speed in dressing is essential and will avoid wasted motions. The dresser may wish to make special notes for accessories and/or props to be carried. A sash, scarf or pin may need to be worn in a certain manner. Simple written directions help to keep the appearance just as it was planned by the fashion coordinator.

Since most clothing used in fashion shows will later be sold, protecting garments is essential. Horror stories about entire racks of clothes falling into slushy snow circulate around fashion offices. While catastrophes of this sort are rare, the dressers need to be concerned with protecting the clothes. Placing a sheet on the floor where the model changes and hanging garments up immediately after they are worn will help to keep the clothes fresh and in good condition. Using a scarf over the model's face will protect clothes from being stained by makeup.

STARTERS

The **starter** is responsible for cueing the models onto the stage in the correct order at the right time using the final lineup or commentary script. The starter should work closely with the commentator at the dress rehearsal and the show. During the rehearsal the starter will make necessary written notes that they will refer to during the show. He or she should know the type of commentary that will be used and the flexibility of the commentator. The commentator's cues will set the pace of the show. The starter will be out of sight of the audience, but will be able to signal the commentator if a model misses her cue in the lineup. The starter will know in advance how fast the models' changes are and will be able to replace a model if she is not ready. At the rehearsal the starter will also be aware of the music and lighting systems to know if the show pace can be altered. The starter is also responsible for the final inspection of the models as they go on stage. Tags should be out of sight, hair smooth, and undergarments concealed.

Minimally, one starter can be used. Depending on the distance between the dressing area and the stage, two or three line personnel should be used, at the stage, at the dressing area, and any area in between where sight and timing are necessary. Communication between the stage and the dressing area is vital. The starter will need to know if a model cannot get changed in time or if an accessory will not be worn with an outfit and alert the commentator. Often communication is in the form of a "runner." The runner moves between the dressing area and the stage to keep all necessary personnel informed of changes so participants can react appropriately. Major fashion shows will have headset contact between all necessary backstage personnel. Whether one or more starters is used, they are vital to the flow of

A dresser works with an individual model or models to assure smooth changes (left). A starter gives a signal for this model to enter the stage (right).

the show. If there is no coordination at the dress rehearsal, the show will not move at the anticipated pace nor will other elements such as music or changes be properly anticipated.

The rehearsal often appears very rough. Participants can be very discouraged at this point, but the rehearsal points out problems that even the most experienced staff may not have anticipated. The staff has the opportunity to rearrange the sequence of models, replace merchandise, perfect timing or solve any other problems that might appear during the rehearsal. The presentation of the show is dependent on the rehearsal, and show personnel always are more confident after the rehearsal.

KEY FASHION SHOW TERMS

dresser	full dress rehearsal	run-through
dress rehearsal	rehearsal	starter

ADDITIONAL READINGS

1. Corinth, *Fashion Showmanship* (1970): The Dressing Room and Its Staff (Chapter 8).

2. Diehl, *How to Produce a Fashion Show* (1970): The Fitting, Run-off and Rehearsal (Chapter 6).

On the Show Day

A fter all of the hours of preparation the show is ready to present. However, prior to the arrival of the audience and models there are a few last-minute details to attend to. Backstage and stage technicalities should be checked and coordinated for things to run smoothly. These checks will help to ensure a smooth, less chaotic presentation.

PREPARING THE BACKSTAGE

The dressing room facilities need to be set up. Mirrors should be available. Racks of clothing should arrive in the dressing area at least two hours prior to the show. The people moving the clothing should be given specific directions as to the delivery location. Although this may seem obvious, there are stories of clothing being delivered to the wrong location.

Lineup sheets should be placed in strategic locations with the dressing room being the number one priority. Lineup sheets should also be available for the starter, commentator, lighting, prop, and music personnel.

Following the steps outlined during the rehearsals, dressers need to organize and prepare clothing and assemble accessories for each model in the order they are to be worn. A final once over of the garments should include pressing and making sure tags are well hidden.

The models should arrive at least thirty minutes to an hour before the start of the show to apply makeup and style their hair before putting on their first outfit.

The commentator should be ready, checking any last minute substitutions in clothing or models at least fifteen to thirty minutes before the show. Commentary cards are placed at the speaker's podium.

The floor plan should be consulted to be sure the stage and runway are ready. Skirting or trim on the runway should be examined. Any set or prop changes should be in place. Cues should be reviewed with the person in charge of set and prop switches. Lighting should also be tested and lighting cues should be reexamined. The sound system should be tested for volume and potential feedback noises before the audience starts to arrive. The commentator's microphone should be tested at the same time music and sound is checked.

Programs are placed on the chairs or tables, or left with the ushers. If hostesses or ushers are going to be used, they must be given instructions. They should be ready at least thirty minutes before the guests arrive. Large charity shows may require elaborate seating arrangements rather than "at large" seating.

Any door prizes or giveaways should be prepared. If a drawing for a gift is going to take place, the procedure for tickets should be ready and in place. A designated person should be responsible for following through with this activity.

Special introductions or oral acknowledgments should be written in advance and rehearsed prior to the audience arrival. The show coordinator, commentator or charity chair may wish to have everyone who took part in the show stand for applause at the end of the show.

If refreshments and food service are to be included as hospitality, they should be placed away from the stage or runway. The audience should not be confused by the service. They should be made aware of when refreshments are to be served, prior to or after the show.

PRESENTING THE SHOW

The opening moments of the show are critical. First impressions will influence the show's success or failure. All of the advance preparation pays off with a show featuring beautiful clothes on attractive models that is well paced with appropriate stage settings, lighting, and music.

It is important to be ready to start the show on time. A five minute delay is not disastrous, but too many shows both professional and amateur start as much as thirty minutes late. If the commentator comes onto the stage at the appointed time and says the show will start in fifteen minutes, the organization looks disorganized and unprofessional and the audience may become restless.

Communication between the commentator or technical assistants has been planned either by eye contact, electronic headsets, or hand signals. There should be visible contact between the commentator and cue, music or lighting personnel. Ideally the commentator should be able to view the area where models will enter. This may help the commentator to gracefully incorporate filler information when the next model is not ready.

Signals to the technical staff may be necessary if there are any problems in that area such as music that may be too loud or soft or if the commentator sounds muffled. The spotlights may be blinding the models or someone in the audience. Even though these points were considered during rehearsal, some conditions may not have been obvious and need to be corrected when the show is underway. A more sophisticated communication system may be required for a fashion show using complex music, lighting, and staging. In this case the headphone system must be used to link dressing room personnel with the technical staff.

The show producers need to be aware of audience reaction throughout the show's production. Audience reaction will reveal technical problems in lighting, sound and music, not detected by show staff. Adjustments in volume of music, public address systems, or lighting may be corrected to make the audience more comfortable. Flexibility is important. Everyone must be able to adjust to the changing conditions.

Cue personnel backstage take direction from the fashion director. Models lineup and enter the stage according to these communications. (*WWD*)

CLOSING THE SHOW

The finale should provide a visual closing to the show. Music and lighting combined with the most dramatic clothing should signal the end of a well-produced fashion show. The end of the show could include some closing remarks by the commentator or show coordinator or the introduction of the designer. A charity show may close with acknowledgments. The show coordinator or commentator may draw the winning tickets for door prizes while the audience watches—all this creates excitement at the end of the show. If refreshments are planned, the audience may be invited to share food or be served.

STAGE STRIKE

A misconception by many people involved in fashion shows is that when the curtain goes down on the show, the show is finished and their responsibilities have been fulfilled. People with this delusion have not yet realized that clean-up and **stage strike** must occur. Stage

Specific areas should be designated for each model in the dressing area (this page, top).

A final touch of hair spray is added to the model as she leaves the dressing area (this page, bottom).

Photographs assist models and dressers with merchandise order and outfit completion (facing page, top right).

Accessory and makeup tables help to keep the backstage area organized (facing page, bottom left).

Some shows will use a makeup artist while other shows will rely on the model to apply her own (facing page, top left and bottom right).

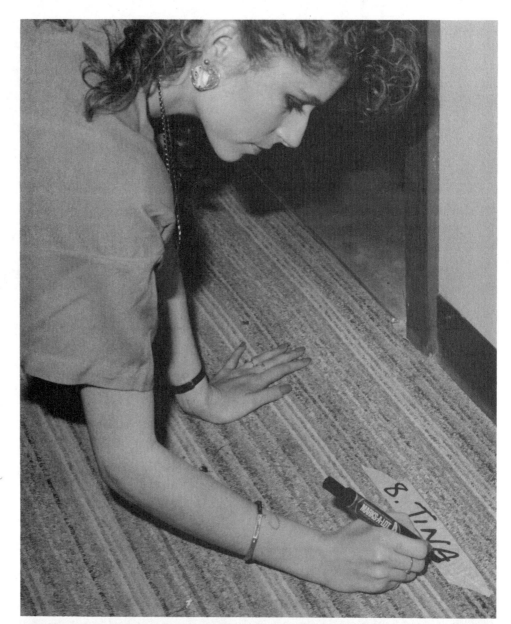

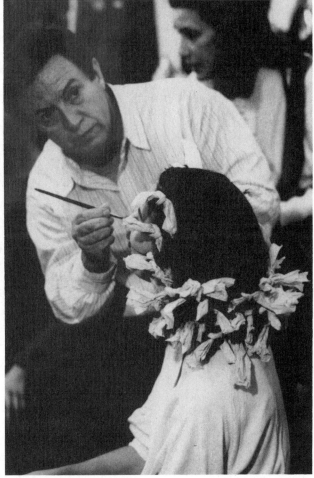

strike, a term taken from the theater, refers to striking the set, physically disassembling the set. Strike takes place at the close of all fashion shows.

In-store strike includes taking down the stage, replacing all props and equipment in the appropriate locations, and leaving the location as it was found. In addition to these activities, a remote show will require transporting the garments and accessories to the selling location.

Retail Shows

Shows within a retail department should be disassembled immediately after the show. Runways should be returned to storage. Backdrops must come down and be stored or disposed of and chairs and tables removed from the selling floor. Retailers frequently have a **prop room** where visual display equipment including props and runways can be stored. Sales areas should be returned to the normal arrangement to accommodate customers anxious to try on the garments. Crowded sales racks must be spaced properly to allow customers to review the merchandise. Safety is a concern within a retail department. With customers wanting to enter the sales area soon after the show it is important to remove props and electrical footage (cords, plugs, and equipment used for the sound system and lights) and secure the area against hazards without delay after the show.

Auditorium Shows

If the show is executed at any location other than a retail department, certain arrangements should have been made with the location personnel and the **staging coordinator** prior to the show. The use of sound equipment and public address systems and the return of these items

Stage hands disassemble
the set after a show.

should have been discussed at the time of location rental. Further, stacking and returning chairs used for audience seating, hostess tables, and skirting for the tables and stage should have been negotiated.

Fashion shows presented in auditoriums or other locations with permanent stages have different requirements during stage strike. Mobile stages, orchestra pit covers, curtains, podiums, lights, and all permanent props of the stage area must be placed in the position where they were situated when show personnel arrived on the site. Sound barriers, often used in auditoriums to bring the action on stage closer to the audience, must be returned to the proper location off stage. Sound barriers are expensive and breakable and should always be moved by stagehands familiar with them. Curtains and orchestra pit covers also require special help from knowledgeable crew personnel in their placement after the show.

If technical assistance is required to dismantle the sound system or lighting systems, the professional technicians used during the show should be responsible for the task. This responsibility should have been discussed with these individuals at the onset of employment and compensation budgeted with all parties in agreement. Rented equipment should be returned as soon as possible after the show to avoid added expenses.

The location of the show should be thoroughly cleaned and left in the order in which it was found. Dressing areas, often rest rooms or offices, should be left in their original state. Programs or giveaways not taken by the audience should be gathered. Pins, tape, tags, and so forth should all be collected by show personnel and not left for the next group to clean up. All trash should be thrown away. The show staff is responsible and must remain at the location until all equipment and garments have been removed. A final check should be completed to make sure no item was left behind.

Personnel

Stage strike should include as many people as possible to make the task easier for everyone. Models and others who are paid hourly may be excused to avoid added costs but all show staff should help. Often in the frenzy of a successful show, many individuals leave the show to review merchandise or celebrate leaving the show coordinator to strike alone. It should be stressed from the planning stages of the show that all individuals will participate in stage strike. Sharp show coordinators turn the task into a fun atmosphere by providing refreshments to an exhausted staff to entice the volunteer crew to stay.

A professional stage crew may be hired to set up and take down the stage. Producers and services may be hired to perform all or some of the following services; set design, stage and runway construction, and lighting design. These services may be available by consulting telephone directories under "Theatrical Equipment and Supplies" or "Theatrical Managers and Producers."

Returning the Merchandise

Garments and accessories should be moved from the show location and returned to the retailers as quickly as possible after the show. The retailers need time to prepare the merchandise for customers who want to try on the garments displayed in the show. If the show is preformed during the daytime, clothing and accessories may be returned before the busi-

Merchandise is immediately returned to the sales area after the show. Shoes must be returned to the department in the condition they were borrowed, ready for sale.

ness day is over. If the show is a night performance, the clothing and accessories may have to be stored at a secure location until the following morning when they can be returned.

Garments should be returned to the retailers in the condition they were borrowed, ready for sale. They should be pressed or steamed, examined for soiling, and hangtags should be replaced. Arrangements for soiled or damaged garments and accessories should have been prearranged with the merchandise coordinator and the retailer in advance of the show.

Garments, upon arrival to the retail store should be inventoried by both the retailer and the merchandise coordinator so both parties are aware of soiled or damaged merchandise. The inventory should be completed and the **merchandise loan record** signed off by the store representative and the show representative. In situations where cleaning is required, the merchandise coordinator should request from the retailer the name of the preferred dry cleaner. If repairs are needed the same policy should be implemented with the retailer's choice of an alterations' service. It is the responsibility of the fashion show personnel to compensate the retailer for any cleaning or repairing that may need to be performed. These expenses should have been included in the budget.

Accessories should also be returned in saleable condition. Accessories including bracelets, necklaces, pins, hair accessories, and scarves should be replaced within the packaging that they were borrowed: cards, boxes, bags, tissue, or other packaging. Some states have health regulations prohibiting the sale of earrings that have been worn. For this reason models often provide their own earrings. The tape applied to shoes should be removed before they are returned. The use of other accessories such as stockings or lingerie which cannot be sold after the show should have been negotiated with the retailer and merchandise coordinator prior to borrowing the merchandise.

SENDING THANK YOU NOTES

Thank you notes should be written as soon as possible after the show. It should be determined in the planning stages of the show who should be responsible for writing the thank you notes. Retailers who loaned merchandise or accessories should be thanked along with other businesses or individuals who provided services or time to the show production. Celebrities or personalities who helped promote the show should also be thanked. Professional models and technicians may not expect a thank you but if the show was an exceptional success it may be a nice gesture on the part of the show staff.

SEDONA SYMPHONY GUILD
423 Lamar
Sedona, Arizona 86336
(602) 282-3521

September 21, 1992

Suzanne Williams
Community Events Director
Sedona Chamber of Commerce
256 Jordan Road
Sedona, AZ 86338

Dear Suzanne:

The Symphony Guild Fashion Show executive committee and I wanted to extend our sincere appreciation for your support of our activities this year! Your serving as our commentator gave an added enthusiasm to the show. Your optimistic attitude and extensive fashion knowledge certainly promoted the fashions from the local merchants who lent clothing to the Symphony Guild.

Thank you so much for helping us. We hope you will join us for a celebration at the guild hall on October 2nd at 8:00 p.m. There is no need to RSVP. We hope to see you there.

Sincerely,

Colleen Doyne
Fashion Show Director

Sample thank you note.

CANCELING A SHOW

It is extremely rare to cancel a fashion show but certain situations call for this action. Severe weather conditions making travel for the audience and staff hazardous is the most likely reason to cancel a show. Announcements should be made through local broadcast media.

Show planners may be hesitant to cancel a program after they have completed so much work putting the show together. The safety and well being of the audience and staff must be a consideration regardless of the effort.

An alternative date may be arranged if a show must be canceled. If this is not possible, refunds should be made available to ticket holders, and somehow expenses must be covered.

PROFESSIONALISM

Professionalism is acting in a manner accepted by the occupation. Simply acting in a manner that respects other people's feelings and respects the merchandise being presented is acting in a professional manner. Planning and executing a fashion show is often done on a tight schedule. Murphy's Law, "whatever can go wrong will go wrong," seems appropriate. Tempers often flare up and personality conflicts often magnify during this stressful time. All participants must keep in mind the goal—a coordinated, well-executed, entertaining fashion show.

The coordinator of the fashion show must be able to diplomatically resolve problems during the planning process and during the production. One important attribute of the fashion show coordinator is tact—the ability to do or say the right thing while not offending anyone.

Flexibility, the ability to adjust to change is also necessary for a successful fashion show. Last minute changes in the merchandise, models forgetting an accessory or prop, garments being soiled or damaged, misplaced music are all a part of fashion show production. Flexibility and a sense of humor help the crew to get through all of the little problems.

Positive working relationships between people involved in fashion show production must be maintained. In a small town many student and civic groups compete with each other to borrow merchandise from local retailers. If the merchandise is not kept in a clean ready to sell condition or not returned in a timely manner, retailers are not likely to continue to allow outside groups to use their merchandise.

A fashion show is just like any theatrical or musical presentation. The audience should not be aware of any of the behind the scenes operations. Backstage should be quiet and efficient in its operation. Members of the audience are likely to enjoy the show, buy merchandise and return to future shows if the quality of the production is at a professional level.

KEY FASHION SHOW TERMS

backstage   merchandise loan record   stage strike
electrical footage   prop room   staging coordinator

ADDITIONAL READINGS

1. Goschie, *Fashion Direction and Coordination* (1986): Execution and Evaluation of
   Fashion Shows (Chapter 8).

Evaluating the Show

The fashion show is not complete until the personnel involved in the production come together one last time to *evaluate* the performance—an aspect of the fashion show often overlooked. Evaluation is the appraising of the performance of people, places, and processes. Because no fashion show is perfect and the personnel involved in future productions may change, notes on procedures and strategies will help the next production crew. While it may seem anticlimactic after the excitement of the actual planning and enactment of the show, an evaluation should be done. Evaluation may minimally include the following topics:

- Type of show presented
- Participants
- Theme and title of the production
- Location
- Audience
- Budget
- Summary of publicity and advertising
- Merchandise
- Models
- Commentary and commentator
- Notes for improvement

Any additional topics may be included for future reference. An **evaluation form** can be used to summarize the evaluation process.

The best time to complete the evaluation process is immediately following the show. It is best to complete the critique as soon as possible since the problems and successes are fresh in everyone's mind. The fashion office of a retail store may decide to hold this meeting the following day. The community group may set a meeting time within a week of the production to evaluate their show.

All the elements in producing a fashion show come together on the day of the show. *(WWD)*

The group evaluating the show should include the people who participated in the production. Any employee of the store or manufacturer not directly involved with the show who viewed the production may be asked for comments. An outside observer such as this, in addition to the audience reaction, can provide an objective perspective. Models, music and lighting technicians could also be asked for constructive comments. If the show was sponsored by a charitable or community association, members of the group should be asked for an opinion.

After the evaluation of the show is completed, the form should be filed with any documentation regarding the planning and presentation of the show—show budget and actual expenses, planning, fitting and model lineup sheets, any correspondence—and kept in a binder or file for reference.

THE EVALUATION PROCESS

Type of Show

The show coordinator or his/her designated representative starts the evaluation process with a discussion regarding the type of show presented. It should include information regarding the extent of the production style. Typical questions to be addressed under this topic might include the following:

- What can be done to improve the format?
- Could the lighting or music be improved?
- Should the same technicians be used for the next show?

Participants

Community clubs and novice fashion show production staffs find it helpful to maintain lists of all people who participated and their responsibilities—including names, addresses and telephone numbers of technicians, models and other outside fashion show production staff. Having a framework of what needs to be done, when and by whom assists in running a future production smoothly. A retailer or manufacturer may not need to keep such a detailed record of participants and their responsibilities because it is part of their job and day-to-day activities.

Theme and Title

The theme and title of the show, any special strategies for capturing the mood of the merchandise and coordinating it with the theme including music, lighting, props or any other devices to enhance the theme are part of the evaluation.

- How did the scenes coordinate with the overall theme?
- Was the theme chosen to correlate with the merchandise?
- Was merchandise readily available to develop the theme and scenes?
- How could the theme be improved?

Location

The location where the fashion show is produced should be thoroughly described. The description should include not only the address but features such as the proximity of the dressing rooms to the show area, seating, accessibility of a runway, helpfulness and cooperation of the restaurant or hotel employees, and any special ambience or amenities. Typical questions relating to the physical location are as follows:

- Was the show presented at the showroom, retail sales floor, a hotel or restaurant?
- Was the facility adequate for the show production staff and the audience?
- Were there any problems getting models from the dressing area to the stage and runway?
- Were the commentator and cue person able to see each other?
- Were there plenty of rest rooms for the audience and show participants?

Figure 14-1

Evaluation Form

EVALUATION FORM

Type of Show

Participants

Theme / Title

Audience

Show Budget (attach Final Budget)

Summary of Publicity and Advertising

Merchandise

Models

Commentary & Commentator

Notes for Improvement

Audience

The audience reaction is one of the most important aspects to be considered in the fashion show evaluation. There are several ways to judge the audience. First the staff should consider the size of the audience.

- Was it appropriate for the dimensions of the space?
- Was it large enough to justify all of the time and expense of producing the show?
- Was it small enough so that every member of the audience could see and enjoy the presentation?

Figure 14-2

Audience Reaction

AUDIENCE REACTION

Age:
- 24 or under ☐   Sex:
- 25-44 ☐   Male ☐
- 45-64 ☐   Female ☐
- 65+ ☐

Family Income:
- $18,999 or under ☐
- $19,000-35,999 ☐
- $36,000-50,999 ☐
- $51,000-65,999 ☐
- $66,000 or more ☐

Rate the Following:

	Like				Dislike
Clothing	☐	☐	☐	☐	☐
Stage Set	☐	☐	☐	☐	☐
Music:					
Style	☐	☐	☐	☐	☐
Loudness	☐	☐	☐	☐	☐
Lighting	☐	☐	☐	☐	☐

How did you find out about the show?
- Newspaper advertisement ☐
- Radio advertisement ☐
- Poster ☐
- Personal Contact ☐
- Other _____
_____
_____

Additional Comments:

It is important to consider the appropriateness of the audience to the merchandise and the type of show produced:
- Was the audience the type desired? If not, why did these people come?
- Was the advertising and promotion campaign targeted to the right group?
- Did the merchandise and theme match the type of audience desired?

Audience reaction is important.
- Was the audience enthusiastic?
- Did they appear to be interested and entertained by the production?
- Did the members of the audience ask where to find the merchandise that was presented?

Frequently fashion show producers evaluate the success of the fashion show as a sales figure. How much of the merchandise presented was actually sold within a specific period of time? This is an oversimplified way to measure the impact of the fashion show. The fashion show can stimulate interest in new apparel. Sales may be encouraged in general themes or categories of merchandise. Purchases may not be for the individual items presented. Customers may be stimulated to buy color trends or new classifications of goods similar to the ones introduced in the show. Increases in store traffic for a retail store or increases in orders at a trade show may be a more effective method of measuring the impact of the show and merchandise.

If the fashion show is presented at a location other than the sales floor, members of the audience may be given a business card offering a discount. The number of people using these cards at the point of sales can help to evaluate audience reaction.

Audience reaction may be evaluated through a questionnaire. Show planners might ask the audience members to comment on demographic information and their attitudes toward aspects of the show such as merchandise selection, lighting, music, and stage set. They might also be asked how they found out about the show.

Budget

Despite careful budgetary planning, the actual expenses may differ from the figures projected in the budget. The actual expenditures should be recorded and compared to the budget. This prospect is important for community groups trying to raise funds for some altruistic or operational project.

- Was the budget realistic?
- What were the unforseen expenses?
- Were there any profits?
- Did ticket sales and donations exceed the costs?

Publicity and Advertising

A recap of the activities relating to advertising and publicity should be included in the show evaluation. Copies of any advertising used, publicity releases, names of media personnel contacted, and any other relevant information can be included in this section. Samples of news articles, advertisements, radio or television spots, programs or flyers can serve as illustrations for the future.

Merchandise

A description of the quantity and types of merchandise presented should be included. It may be helpful to include the length of time required to show the number of outfits presented. This could serve as a guideline for future timing.

Fitting sheets and scene charts could enhance this basic information. The relationship of the merchandise to the scene theme and fashion show theme can be discussed.

- Was the merchandise appropriate to the theme, audience and company image?
- What departments participated in a retail show?
- Were any departments that should have been included overlooked?

An informal show was planned to introduce the Ralph Lauren Polo Shop at Saks Fifth Avenue, New York. (*WWD*)

Models

The names, addresses and telephone numbers of the models featured in the show should be recorded. Accounts of the models performance will be beneficial in selecting models for future work.

- Did any of the models have problems such as stage fright or trouble changing in the time allowed?
- Were the models on time?
- Were the models cooperative or hard to get along with?

Commentary and Commentator

Copies of the commentary should be included in the fashion show evaluation.

- Was it interesting?
- Did the commentary avoid being too descriptive of the garments?
- Did the commentary flatter and strengthen the theme of the show?
- Was the commentator effective in his/her delivery?

Notes for Improvement

Identify strategies that worked well. Keep these techniques fresh for the future. It is just as important to note things that did not function properly. For example, if the cue person could not see the models, he or she could not give suitable entrance signals. How could visibility be improved?

Measuring Success

It is difficult to measure the success of any particular show. Some people gauge the achievement by the dollar volume of the sales, others assess the accomplishment by the reaction of the audience and participants. No matter how success is defined, producing a fashion show can be an exciting and rewarding experience.

A fashion show is not truly over until the staff completes an evaluation. Looking at the successes and problems will help ease some of the stress when the staff produces their next show.

KEY FASHION SHOW TERMS

evaluation form   evaluation process

ADDITIONAL READINGS

1. Goschie, *Fashion Direction and Coordination* (1986): Execution and Evaluation of Fashion Shows (Chapter 8).

Glossary of Fashion Show Terms

advance planning Organizing the show, including selecting leadership, delegating responsibilities, foreseeing problems which may occur, and continually reviewing the progress of the show.

advertising Information paid for and controlled by the sponsoring organization.

advertising unit Space designated in print media by column inch.

amateur models Models not trained as professional models; available from a variety of resources.

apparel marts Wholesale centers located in major cities throughout the United States leasing space to manufacturers who are able to offer their lines closer to the retailer's geographic location.

art Illustrations or photography of the advertisement.

audience The accumulation of spectators to view the show.

body Important details of the advertisement or news article.

booking Scheduling a model through an agency.

British Designer Shows One of the two main British designer shows.

budget An estimate of the revenues and expenses necessary to produce the fashion show.

budgetary process Advance budget planning for the operating season which includes appropriating funds for promotional activities.

Camera Nazionale della Alta Moda Italia The governing body of the Italian couture overseeing the activities of couture designers, ready-to-wear, shoe and accessory manufacturers.

Chambre Syndicale de la Couture Parisienne The trade organization of the French couture.

child models Youngsters engaged for presenting clothing and accessories for the toddler to preteen markets in addition to the important back-to-school season.

choreographer Individual in charge of planning runway and dance routines.

choreography All of the planning and execution of the model's runway routines as well as any specific dance numbers used in a fashion show.

clip art Prefabricated illustrations generated on a computer or purchased in clip art books.

commentary Oral delivery of descriptive details of fashion show garments and accessories.

commentary cards Fragments of information prepared to read as narration during the show usually on a file card.

commentator Member of the show staff with the designated responsibility of preparing and/or delivering the commentary during the show.

consumer fashion show Show presented to the ultimate consumer, the person who buys garments and accessories for his or her personal use.

copy Written material in a press release or advertisement.

copyright permission Authorization from the owner of the copyright to use copyrighted materials.

couturier/couturiere A French term referring to the male or female designer or proprietor of a couture house.

created audience Individuals who will attend as a result of publicity and advertising.

cue Signal on or off the stage for an entrance.

 D

dancing Routines or rhythmic movements to music which can add a great deal of interest to the show.

Defiles des Createurs Designer runway shows in Paris featuring French, Italian, American, Japanese, and other international designers.

design piracy Stealing designs and creating "knock-offs".

designer shows A ready-to-wear manufacturer's show featuring a well-known designer.

diary Written record of all plans for the show.

direct advertising Materials left on counter or desk tops for people to pick up.

direct mail Advertising sent through the mail.

directrice/directeur A French term referring to the male or female head of the couture salon.

disk jockey Individual who uses playback equipment to play music.

documentary videos Videos that focus on the designer or behind-the-scenes activities of the manufacturer.

door prizes Gifts given to selected members of the audience as an acknowledgement for purchasing a ticket.

dramatized show See production show.

dress rehearsal A walk-through with garment changes.

dressers Individual responsible for helping the models change.

 E

electrical footage Cords, plugs and equipment used for the sound and lighting systems.

emcee A master of ceremonies.

evaluation Appraisal of the performance, people, places and processes.

evaluation form A document used to summarize the evaluation process.

F

fashion advisory boards Advisory panels organized by retailers to obtain consumer information about the store. Board members may be asked to serve as advisors regarding merchandise and services, salespersons or models for fashion shows.

Fashion Calendar A calendar published weekly with the dates and relevant information regarding key national and international fashion events serving as a guide for retailers, manufacturers and the press.

fashion director Individual responsible for creating the fashion image for a particular retailer. He or she is responsible for selecting silhouettes, colors, and fabrics for the upcoming seasons and establishing a sense of fashion leadership for the store to the public.

fashion dolls Miniature scale dolls wearing replicas of the latest clothing. One of the first forms of transmitting fashion information to potential consumers, were also known as puppets, dummies, little ladies or fashion babies.

fashion editor Individual at a newspaper, exclusively responsible for fashion. Usually the contact person for fashion show producers.

fashion parade See formal runway show.

fashion show The presentation of apparel, accessories, and other products to enhance personal attractiveness on live models to an audience.

fashion show coordinator Individual charged with the responsibility of producing the show, planning all arrangements, delegating responsibilities, and accepting accountability for all details.

fashion show plan The schedule for a specific period of time, commonly six months or a year, of all the fashion shows that a firm intends to produce.

fashion show videos Documentation of designer, manufacturer or retail store fashion shows onto videotape.

fashion trend show A detailed fashion forecast for the two major seasons: fall/winter and spring/summer provided by the fashion director.

Federation Française du Prêt-à-porter Feminin Scheduling organization for the Paris ready-to-wear shows.

filler commentary Commentary planned for use at any time during the show to fill in unexpected pauses which may occur.

finale The last impression of the show.

final lineup A complete listing of models and outfits in order of appearance, finalized after the dress rehearsal.

fit models Models of sample size who work in a manufacturer's design area. Sample garments are adjusted to a standard fit model's size.

fittings Matching models to merchandise which are planned and held when the tentative lineup is completed.

fitting sheet An information sheet coordinated to the merchandise, including sizing, order number, and detailed description of the garment.

formal runway show A conventional presentation of fashion that is similar to a parade. This kind of fashion show may also be called a fashion parade. It features a series of models who walk or dance on a runway in a sequential manner.

full commentary Commentary written word for word on cards or in script form prior to the show.

full dress rehearsal A rehearsal with garment changes to check all aspects of the show including timing, music and all other technical aspects.

G

garment tag Label containing model's name, brief description of the garment and the category number.

giveaways Small items given to every audience member.

go see Initial visit of a professional model to a potential client.

grouping Coordinating merchandise within categories using style characteristics, color, or fabrication to achieve a balance and rhythm.

guaranteed audience Individuals who will attend the show regardless of the fashions displayed.

halftone illustrations Reproduced photographs or drawings using screens to convert the design into a series of dots, making shaded values in printing possible.

hatbox show Fashion show involving a single person presenting the show by modeling an outfit then moving behind a screen to change into another outfit. The individual maintains a commentary while changing clothes.

haute couture The French high fashion industry featuring clothing produced from a client's made-to-order measurements as well as items sold to other manufacturers and retailers. The couture shows are held in January and July each year.

headline Part of an advertisement or news article used to attract the attention of the reader and create interest.

headsheets Model books provided by the agency to enable fashion show producers to evaluate the look and experience of the professional models prior to an initial visit called a "go see."

high fashion models A limited number of highly paid women who are internationally known and work for the top international and domestic designers. Models are typically 18 to 35 years old and a minimum of 5' 8" tall.

ideal chart Plan listing all categories of merchandise which will be represented in the show, including important trends or looks that should be in each category.

impromptu commentary Commentary created spontaneously during the show using only brief cue cards for assistance.

individual model lineup sheet A form used in organizing the specific model's order of appearance, outfit, shoes, hosiery, accessories, props and grouping.

informal fashion show A casual presentation of garments and accessories. No theatrical elements such as music, lighting or runway are used.

institutional advertising Promotion enhancing the store image.

in-store training fashion show Type of fashion show most often presented in the morning before the store is opened to train store personnel coinciding with the seasonal trend show.

instructional video Videos created for in-store training of sales personnel or store customers. Current information on fashion trends and special features of the products are shown.

instrumental music Music created from instruments without words.

junior models Young models who are between the ages of 13 and 17.

knock-offs Copies of designer originals at lower prices.

layout Blueprint for the placement and size of the elements of the advertisement.

lease agreements Contracts between leasing agencies and users drawn up prior to the show.

line drawing Illustration created by pen, pencil, brush, or crayon.

lineup An organized listing of the models, the order in which they will appear and the outfit they will be wearing.

live mixed music The use of a disk jockey and playback equipment to change music during various segments of the show.

live music A performance provided by musicians during the show.

local broadcast advertising Time bought on local television stations.

logo A copyright protected symbol or phrase used by an incorporated organization.

London Designer Collections One of the two main British designer shows.

M

magazine tie-in Cooperative fashion shows between major fashion publications such as *W, Vogue, Glamour* or *Mademoiselle* and individual retailers.

male models Men who are hired to display clothing and accessories and have been important to the production of fashion shows since the 1960s.

mannequin modeling Modeling involving live models in a store window or on a display platform. These models strike similar poses to the stationary display props for which they have been named.

mannequins Live models used to present merchandise in fashion shows. The House of Worth was the first to use mannequins in this manner. Prior to this mannequin referred to a stationary doll or dummy used as a display fixture.

manufacturer's fashion show Show used to introduce a new line to retail buyers, media or a national sales force. The manufacturer's show is presented during market week.

mapped routes Paths planned for models to follow on the runway.

market week The time designated for producers of a specific category of merchandise to open sales on the season's new styles.

media list A locally or regionally generated list of media, which might be used to publicize an event.

merchandise categories Divisions of merchandise, often corresponding with retail departments.

merchandise loan record Standardized form used by fashion show producers to record details of the merchandise borrowed from retailers. The loan record should include a description of the garment, manufacturer, color, size, price, time of loan, store authorization, department location, and when it will be returned and who will be responsible for the return of the merchandise.

merchandise pull Physically removing merchandise from the sales floor to an area reserved for fashion show merchandise storage.

merchandise selection Designation of current stock for presentation in a fashion show.

missy models Models generally between the ages of 17 to 22 years of age. These women are between 5' 7" and 5' 10½". They wear the sample sizes from 6 or 8..

model An individual employed to display clothing and accessories by wearing them.

model agencies Companies that represent and act as scheduling agents for a variety of fashion models.

model card An information card that provides specific characteristics about each model, including model's name, height, and shoe, hosiery and foundation sizes.

model coordinator Individual responsible for selecting and training the models, and coordinating activities that involve the models.

modeling schools Schools that train men, women and children in modeling techniques. Classes may involve such activities as runway methods, makeup application for photography or runway, hairstyling, voice, figure control, and new modeling procedures.

model list A form that will include the model's name, telephone number, garment and shoe sizes.

model order Rotation in which the models will appear throughout the show.

music The vocal and instrumental sound environment.

music director Employee who will research and select the appropriate music, obtain permissions to use copyrighted music, mix the music at the show, and prepare the sound system at the show site.

music mix The combination of different musical styles to create a specified mood.

music technician An expert in musical styles and sound systems.

national promotion Primary and secondary sales promotion activities directed at the ultimate consumer.

network advertising Time bought on one of the three major networks.

new store opening A fashion show introducing the store, personnel and merchandise to the public.

no show Model that does not fulfill obligation by not showing up for a rehearsal or show.

nonprofit organization An organization with 501 c3 status as designated by the Internal Revenue Service with published articles of incorporation, a board of directors and all money earned by the organization is returned to the group.

pace Timing of the show.

partial commentary Commentary written providing major details about the outfit. The description of the fashions and accessories are stated impromptly by the commentator as needed.

paste-up All elements of an advertisement placed in final arrangement, camera ready.

pauses Planned hesitations when models stop and pose on the runway.

personal image and wardrobe consulting A fashion show presenting general trends and fashion analysis for a particular body type.

personal selling The direct interaction between the customer and the seller with the purpose of making a sale.

petite models Models approximately 5' 2" wearing special sizes.

photography Reproduction of prints created by a camera.

pivots Turns executed by models on the runway.

planning sheet The initial list of music selections including title and length of the song and the recording artist(s).

plus size models Full figure models with the following physical characteristics; height 5'7", bust 44½", waist 36", and hips 47".

point-of-purchase video Videos placed on the sales floor of a retail store. Consumers are given the opportunity to see the original manufacturer's runway show or an action view of how to wear the merchandise.

posters Signs (8½" x 14: or 11" x 17") read easily and quickly from a distance, promoting a product or event.

preferred position Newspaper advertisement run at a specified page or position within the newspaper.

premier/premiere A French term referring to the male or female head of the couture workroom.

press kit A collection of materials delivered or mailed to the press in a folder with inside pockets. Contents include press releases, news stories, feature stories, fact sheets, photographs with captions, biographical or historical information about the event or people involved, and brochures or samples.

press photographs Photographs prepared specifically for use in print media to accompany press releases or as part of a press kit.

press release Written article about a newsworthy event in a specified format, including all details about the event, sent to editors or news directors, for publication in the media.

press show A fashion show held specifically for the press to preview the fashions before public viewing. Editors, broadcast news directors, other members of the press, buyers, and special invited guests or important customers are invited to press shows.

prêt-à-porter The ready-to-wear fashion industry in France.

primary resources Manufacturers involved with the production of raw materials including textile fibers, fabrics, trims and notions.

prime time Radio drive time is in the mornings and evenings: 6:00 to 9:00 A.M. and 4:00 to 7:00 P.M. Television prime time is viewing time evenings from 7:00 to 10:00.

production show The most dramatic or theatrical production type. The production fashion show may also be called a dramatized or spectacular show. The fashion trends are emphasized using special entertainment, backdrops or scenery, lighting effects, live or specially produced music, and perhaps dancing or specialized choreography during this most elaborate and expensive fashion show.

professionalism Acting in a manner accepted by the position and/or occupation.

professional models Models trained in modeling techniques and hired through model agencies or modeling schools.

program editor Individual responsible for all activities related to creating a program.

programs Guides with a brief description of the ensemble being shown in their show order.

promotional advertising Promotion for the specific purpose of selling products.

promotion coordinator Individual responsible for the creation and distribution of promotional materials required for the show.

prop room Space where visual display equipment including props and runways can be stored.

props Items or symbols used in fashion shows to highlight the garments exhibited.

public address system Microphone, amplifiers, and speakers used to project voices.

publicity The non-paid, un-sponsored information delivered at the discretion of the media initiated by the party seeking to tell others about the event.

public relations (PR) The interrelationship between service providers and the public, as it relates to the image of the organization through all levels of communication.

public service announcements (PSA's) Radio spots run free of charge to charitable organizations to deliver a message about their organization or benefit.

rate card Published rates for advertising units in print media.

rate costs The cost of advertising during a specified period of time in a specified media.

rehearsal The practice performance, held in private, in preparation for a public performance. The rehearsal is the opportunity for the fashion show coordinator to solve any problems prior to the public presentation of the show.

responsibility sheet A form used in planning a show and delegating responsibilities to all participants.

retail promotion Store promotion directed at the consumer.

runway The extension of the walkway that generally projects into the audience.

run-of-paper position (R.O.P. rate) Newspaper advertisement run at any location in the newspaper.

run-through The rehearsal of the show sequence. This involves showing the models the choreography. This type of rehearsal does not require wearing the clothing for the show.

sales promotion Any activity used to help deliver the product from the producer to the consumer. These activities include advertising, fashion shows, personal selling, publicity, public relations, special events, and visual merchandising.

script commentary Commentary used in production shows, written out word for word for the commentator to read and speak like that of a broadcast. Scripts are written with two columns, denoting technical cues and spoken commentary with planned pauses.

secondary resources Clothing and accessory manufacturers.

senior model Model at least 40 years of age with a youthful appearance.

signage In-store visual identification of information in a written form.

slogan A catchy phrase which is appealing when spoken or viewed in print.

sound library A collection of records, cassettes, and/or CD's to be used by the public.

sound system Equipment needed to play music.

special events Activities sponsored by retailers to attract customers to their store while creating goodwill.

specialty market shows Shows geared to a specific, narrowly defined, group of consumers, such as petite or plus sizes or special interests like bridal or back-to-school.

spectacular show See production show.

spot advertising Time bought on independently owned broadcast stations.

stage The background area where the models enter and exit. It may be decorated with a designer, retailer or manufacturer's logo or some type of scene theme.

stage manager Individual responsible for organizing the equipment and people providing services used behind the scenes.

stage strike Physically disassembling the set.

staging coordinator See stage manager.

standard Newspaper format 6 columns wide and 26½ inches high.

starter Individual responsible for "cueing" the models to go on stage in the correct order at the right time.

subheadline Part of advertisement or news article that further explains the headline.

table seating Seating arrangements used at a show with some sort of meal service. A buffet or sit down meal could be served prior to or after the fashion show.

tabloid Newspaper format 5 columns wide and 14 inches high.

taped music Pre-recorded music from records, cassettes, and/or CD's, copied to tape.

tea-room modeling Modeling at restaurants featuring fashions from a local retail store.

tear sheet An advertisement torn directly from the newspaper to show proof of publication to the advertiser.

tentative lineup Order of models and merchandise designed from the groupings without input from fittings.

tertiary resources Retail organizations.

theatrical seating Chairs placed side by side next to the stage and runway. This type of seating is best used for fashion shows without meal service.

theme The title of the show indicating the nature of the fashion show to the audience.

trade Any activity aimed at distribution of fashion and related products within the industry. Trade shows, also called industrial shows, are produced to sell raw materials to manufacturers or manufactured goods to retailers.

trade associations Groups of individuals and businesses acting as a professional, nonprofit collective in meeting common interests. Membership in trade associations provides a means for information exchange and political action to benefit the public opinion and legislative concerns.

trade promotion Activities designed to promote products from one business to another. This type of promotional activity involves patronage from a primary resource to a secondary producer or retailer or from a secondary producer to a retailer.

trade shows A group of manufacturers presenting their lines to retailers and press one to four times each year. Some shows are exclusive to one product line while others may involve several categories of merchandise.

training fashion shows Shows produced specifically to educate employees of trends and promotions for a given season.

transit media Billboards, above-the-seat subway or bus signage, signage on bus stop benches or other outside locations which commuters pass as they are in transit.

trickle-down theory The theory of fashion adoption where items are first presented at higher prices to a limited audience and later adopted at lower prices by a larger audience.

trunk show A specific type of informal fashion show that features garments from one manufacturer or designer at a retail store. The manufacturer's or designer's complete line is shipped to a store in "trunks" or sales representative's cases.

video production Use of video technology to record fashion shows or special events. These tapes would be used in training the national sales force or be presented to retailers to show in their stores. Three types of video productions are point-of-purchase, instructional and documentary.

visual merchandising The physical presentation of products in a nonpersonal approach, including window, interior or remote displays.

vocal music Music with words sung.

white space Space between the copy and art of an advertisement.

Glossary of People Who Influenced the Fashion Show

Bertin, Rose (1747-1813) French dressmaker to be recognized by name; achieved international fame as dressmaker to Marie Antoinette and distributer of fashion dolls. Known as the *Minister of Fashion.*

Chanel, Gabrielle (1883-1971) First French designer to distribute photographs to the press prior to collection openings. She maintained the traditional fashion parade as a method of presenting couture collections from the 1920s to the 1970s.

Chase, Edna Woolman (1877-1957) Editor of *Vogue* Magazine credited with originating the fashion trade show in 1914 when Vogue produced a charitable benefit, called the "Fashion Fete", sponsored by society leaders.

de Wolfe, Elsie (1865-1950) Decorator and international socialite involved in selection of American models for the House of Patou.

Ellis, Perry (1940-1986) American Designer who set a precedent for using photographic models for runway shows, blurring the distinction between photographic and runway models in the 1970s.

Maxwell, Elsa Popular party planner of the 1920s who acted as the first press agent for House of Patou.

Nast, Condé (1873-1942) Publisher of *Vogue* Magazine since 1909 who assisted in the selection of American models for House of Patou among his many contributions to fashion history.

Quant, Mary (1934-) British designer who revolutionized fashion shows in the 1960s by having models dance to contemporary music among other innovative ideas.

Paquin, House of Founded in 1891. Mme. Paquin, French designer, known for parading models at the racetrack and opera during the 1920s. She introduced the tableau or finale for her events. House closed, 1956.

Patou, Jean (1887-1936) First French designer to schedule a special preview showing of his collection to representatives of the press, notable buyers and exceptional clients before his regular opening. Also known for bringing American fashion models to Paris to model his collection in 1925.

Poiret. Paul (1879-1944) French designer with a knack for promotion. He toured making personal appearances at chic resorts with his mannequins to present his collection from as early as 1912.

Steichen, Edward (1879-1973) Innovative fashion photographer who assisted in the selection of the American models for the House of Patou.

Worth, Charles Frederick (1825-1895) British-born, French fashion innovator who created the first couture house in Paris in 1858. First designer to use mannequins in his showroom; also known as the *Father of Haute Couture*.

Bibliography

Books

American Psychological Association. *Publication Manual of the American Psychological Association*. Washington, D.C., 1983.

Basic Sales Promotion Procedures for Apparel Retailers. Oklahoma State University, Center for Apparel Marketing, 1986.

Blue, M. *Making it Legal*. Flagstaff, AZ: Northland Press, 1988.

Calasibetta, C. M. *Fairchild's Dictionary of Fashion*, 2nd edition. New York: Fairchild Publications, 1988.

Chase, E. W. and I. Chase. *Always in Vogue*. New York: Doubleday & Company, Inc., 1954.

Corinth, K. *Fashion Showmanship*. New York: John Wiley & Sons, 1970.

Diehl, M. E. How to Produce a Fashion Show. New York: Fairchild Publications, 1976.

Edelman, A, H. *The Fashion Resource Directory*, 2nd edition. New York: Fairchild Publications, 1991.

Etherington-Smith, M. *Patou*. New York: St. Martin's Press, 1984.

Frings, G. S. *Fashion: from Concept to Consumer*, 2nd edition. Englewood Cliffs, NJ: Prentice Hall, 1986.

Goschie, S. *Fashion Direction and Coordination*, 2nd edition. Mission Hills, CA: Glencoe, 1986.

Guerin, P. *Creative Fashion Presentations*. New York: Fairchild Publications, 1987.

Guerin, P. *Fashion Writing*. Indianapolis: Bobbs-Merrill, 1972.

Jabenis, E. *The Fashion Directors: What They do and How to Become One*, 2nd edition. New York: Macmillan, 1983.

Jernigan, M. H. and C. Easterling. *Fashion Merchandising and Marketing*. New York: Macmillan, 1990.

Kemp, J. E. and D. C. Smelli. *Planning, Producing, and Using Instructional Media*, 6th edition. New York: Harper & Row, 1989.

Lenz, B. *The New Complete Guide of Fashion Modeling*. New York: Crown Publishers, 1982.

Madsen, A. *Chanel: A Woman of Her Own*. New York: Henry Holt, 1990.

McDowell, C. *McDowell's Directory of Twentieth Century Fashion*. New York: Prentice Hall, 1987.

Moor, J. *Perry Ellis*. New York: St. Martin's Press, 1988.

O'Brien, R. *Publicity: How to Get It*. New York: Harper & Row, 1977.

Perna, R. *Fashion Forecasting*. New York: Fairchild Publications, 1987.

Producing Fashion Shows. Oklahoma State University, Center for Apparel Marketing, 1986.

Quant, M. *Quant by Quant*. London: Cassell, 1965.

Stegemeyer, A. *Who's Who in Fashion*. New York: Fairchild Publications, 1988.

_____. Who's Who in Fashion, 2nd edition, Supplement. New York: Fairchild Publications, 1991.

Train, Susan, editor. *Theatre de la mode*. New York: Rizzoli Publishers, 1991.

Winters, A. A. and S. Milton. *The Creative Connection*. New York: Fairchild Publications, 1982.

Winters, A. A. and S. Goodman. *Fashion Advertising & Promotion*, 6th edition. New York: Fairchild Publications, 1984.

Periodical Articles

Balavender, R. "Clues from the Collections." *Visual Merchandising & Store Design*, July 1990, pp. 18-22.

Boyes, K. "SA's Sound of Music." *Women's Wear Daily*, February 26, 1990, pp. 26-27.

Darnton, N. "French Fashion Goes Global." *Newsweek*, November 6, 1989, p. 75.

_____. "Show Enough." *Newsweek*, April 2, 1990, pp. 62-64.

Deeny, G. "On the Runways: The $50 Million Fashion Machine." *W*, October 14-21, 1991, pp. 82-84.

Fitzgerald, S. "The Countless Steps Leading to the Runway." *Newsday*, May 12, 1983, pp. 8-11.

Gross, M. "Slave of Fashion." *New York Magazine*, October 1, 1990, pp. 32-39.

"Harem's Full Trunk." *Women's Wear Daily* (Supplement: Best of Group III), August 1990, p. 34.

Haynes, K. "Campbell Scoop." *Women's Wear Daily*, August 10, 1990, p. 16.

"Outdoor Advertising." *Ready-to-Wear Review*, August 1990, p. 3.

"The Outdoors Allure." *Ready-to-Wear Review*, August 1990, p. 3.

"Rules of the Game." *Women's Wear Daily*, January 18, 1990, p. 5.

"When the Show Goes On." *Vogue Magazine*, February 1984, p. 294.

Visuals

Guerin, Polly. Creative Fashion Presentations (slides and videotape). New York: Fairchild Visuals, 1988.

Index